The Art of Political Framin

The Art of Political Framing

How Politicians Convince Us That They Are Right

Hans de Bruijn

LONDON AND NEW YORK

First published in 2019 by Amsterdam University Press Ltd.

Published 2025 by Routledge
4 Park Square, Milton Park, Abingdon, Oxon OX14 4RN
605 Third Avenue, New York, NY 10158

Routledge is an imprint of the Taylor & Francis Group, an informa business

© H. de Bruijn / Taylor & Francis Group 2019

All rights reserved. No part of this book may be reprinted or reproduced or utilised in any form or by any electronic, mechanical, or other means, now known or hereafter invented, including photocopying and recording, or in any information storage or retrieval system, without permission in writing from the publishers.

Trademark notice: Product or corporate names may be trademarks or registered trademarks, and are used only for identification and explanation without intent to infringe.

ISBN: 9789463721127 (pbk)
ISBN: 9781003705314 (ebk)
NUR 754

Cover design: Gijs Mathijs Ontwerpers

DOI: 10.5117/9789463721127

For Product Safety Concerns and Information please contact our EU representative: GPSR@taylorandfrancis.com
Taylor & Francis Verlag GmbH, Kaufingerstraße 24, 80331 München, Germany

Contents

Part One   Language and Framing

1. Language matters — 9
2. What is framing and how does it work? — 19

Part Two   Strategies

3. The 3P model — 39
4. Victims, villains, and heroes — 53
5. Playing with your opponent's values — 67
6. Playing with opposite perspectives — 79
7. Meta-framing — 101
8. Emotion and monopolies on emotion — 115

Part Three   Reflection

9. How should we value the game of framing and reframing? — 129

Notes — 135

References — 139

Part One

Language and Framing

1. Language matters

Josiah Bartlet and his language plan

At the turn of the century, the popular and well-received HBO series *The West Wing* tells the story of a fictional Democratic president, Josiah Bartlet, and his staff.

Half-way through Bartlet's second term, the American economy is in bad shape, putting Bartlet on the defensive in the public debate. His advisors are concerned about the White House's "lack of vocabulary." The president decides to take action:

> Okay,
> let's get on
> coming up with a language plan.[1]

Bartlet needs a plan, not about his strategy or policy, but about the language he should use. Evidently, language matters in politics. In this book I will examine how politicians use language when they participate in political debates, try to shape our opinions, or challenge their opponents' positions. But first the question is: why does language matter?

Why language matters in the world of politics

Politicians employ a wide range of strategies to achieve their goals – and language is one of them. What impact does their language have on us, on their opponents, on the public opinion?

Language shapes our perception of the world

In a well-known experiment, two groups of people are instructed to analyze the crime figures for a fictional city called Addison.[2] They are then asked to describe what strategy the authorities should adopt to make the city safer. The language used in the instructions is different for each group. Group 1 is told that crime is like a predator lurking in an increasing number of neighborhoods, while Group 2 is told that crime is like a virus infecting an increasing number of neighborhoods. Both groups are then asked to analyze the numerical data and identify the best way to tackle the problem.

It turns out that the wording of the assignment affects the respondents' interpretation of the data. If crime is a predator, the natural response is to hunt it down. The first group accordingly opts for stronger enforcement. On the other hand, if crime is a virus, the natural response is to attack it at the source. The second group of respondents accordingly believes that efforts should focus on the causes of crime, such as poverty and lack of educational opportunities. One might be inclined to think that this is an obvious outcome given the heavy-handed nature of the metaphors employed. In a follow-up experiment, the instructions therefore refer only once to the predator or the virus, while the rest of the instructions consists of a detailed technical description of the case. In spite of this, the outcome is the same. Language shapes the way in which the respondents perceive the world.

Next – and this is where things really get interesting – the respondents are asked why they had chosen either approach. They all respond that their choice is based solely on the crime figures. The wording of the instructions has thus become the filter through which the respondents perceive the facts, but they are unaware of this. They think that their opinions are based on objective numerical data. This has enormous implications. Politicians who are able to impose their language can make us perceive the world through a specific filter without us even realizing it.

Language not only describes, but also creates a reality

In 1984, Stan Greenberg observes that many voters who have always voted Democrat had switched sides to Ronald Reagan's

Republicans.³ He calls them Reagan Democrats. In doing so, he not only describes a reality but creates one as well. A new group of voters is called into existence as a result of this label, and this activates an entirely new dynamic. Journalists become interested in these Reagan Democrats and want to know why they have abandoned the Democratic Party. Discussions arise about their political positioning. Where is Reagan Democrat country? Winning back the Reagan Democrats becomes a key strategic issue for the Democrats. Without Greenberg's label, this group of voters would never have received so much attention.

A more recent example of this phenomenon: after 9/11, several right-wing populist parties with a strong anti-Islamic stance emerge in northwestern Europe. They introduce the term "Islamization," to describe Islam's increasing influence in Europe and the continent's transformation into "Eurabia" due to an influx of Islamic migrants.⁴ The populist parties constantly talk about the Islamization of Europe, and the term has become so accepted that even their opponents have started using it. Once people look at the world through this filter, anybody who believes Islamization is really happening will start seeing it everywhere. Women wearing scarves, halal butchers, and an inflammatory sermon delivered by an imam, all serve to confirm that Europe is undergoing a process of Islamization.

Language thus both describes and creates reality. By the same token, a lack of vocabulary also has serious implications. The medical community's understanding of cancer and the number of available treatments have increased significantly in recent decades. However, according to several leading American scientists, the language we use to describe cancer is still stuck in the nineteenth century. Scans sometimes detect tumors that will probably not cause the patient any problems but are still referred to as "cancer." This dated and unsophisticated language has serious consequences, in that it causes needless anxiety and often leads to overtreatment, which is dangerous for patients and occasionally results in permanent harm. The American scientists therefore propose using more sophisticated language to describe cancer, including the term "indolent lesions of epithelial origin" (IDLEs) for slow-growing or low-risk tumors.⁵ Calling such tumors IDLEs rather than cancer can create an entirely different reality for patients.

Language evokes connotations – positive or negative

In the 1960s, left-wing politicians, in particular, develop proposals for providing every citizen with a government-funded *guaranteed minimum income*. Some right-wing politicians are also in favor of this idea, but the concept of a "guaranteed minimum income," especially one provided by the state, has too many left-wing, big-government connotations for their tastes. They therefore refer to it as a "negative income tax," which obviously sounds much better to right-wing voters. In most countries, the idea never took off, but a few decades later it finds its way back on to the political agenda. This time, anybody wishing to avoid associations with the 1960s did not refer to it as a "guaranteed minimum income" but as a "citizen's income."

Guaranteed minimum income, *negative income tax* and *citizen's income* are all roughly the same thing, but they have very different connotations. Those connotations matter, since they shape our judgments.⁶ Here are a few more examples of words with powerful connotations.

Development aid: US president Jimmy Carter observes that the term "development aid" has negative connotations in the United States.⁷ Anyone who tries to promote the issue immediately shoots himself in the foot by using this word. Instead, you could talk about "investments" in "emerging economies."

Compromise: Throughout his tenure as the Republican Speaker of the House of Representatives during the Obama presidency, John Boehner refuses to use the word "compromise." "When you say the word 'compromise,' a lot of Americans look up and go, 'Uh-oh, they're going to sell me out.' And so 'finding common ground' I think makes more sense," he explains in an interview.⁸ For Europeans, who are accustomed to coalition governments, this may seem like a strange position, but for American conservatives "compromise" appears to be dangerous language.

Christians: In 2015, ISIS militants murder a group of Egyptian Coptic Christians in Libya. In a statement concerning the incident, the US State Department describes the victims as "Egyptian citizens" and does not refer to them as "Christians."[9] It chooses to do so because any mention of the victims' religion would only serve to reinforce the narrative that ISIS is seeking to impose on the conflict in Iraq and Syria, namely that it is involved in a "clash of civilizations," a struggle between Islam and Christian crusaders.

Deportation: US politicians talk about "deporting" illegal immigrants, but such language is unacceptable in Europe because of its connotations with the mass deportation – and extermination – of Jews there during World War II. European politicians therefore prefer to use other terms, such as "repatriation" or "return."

Language influences value judgments

Words instantly evoke certain connotations, including moral connotations. As a consequence of that, language can also be used to convey and influence value judgments.

The former French politician Dominique Strauss Kahn liked it to visit a "libertine evening." According to others, he is talking about an orgy. A libertine evening or an orgy – the words might evoke completely different connotations. Is a country faced with "illegal immigrants" or "undocumented workers"? When immigrants have obtained the right papers and their families join them – is this "family reunification" or "chain migration"? You can disqualify a peer who has comments on your work as "cynical" – although this peer is merely "critical." Is a manager "downsizing" or "rightsizing" an organization? "Reorganizing" or "modernizing"? Some politicians says that they are "realistic" – that they accept that refugees from war-torn zones will keep coming to the rich and free democratic world. No, say their opponents – you are not realistic, you are "fatalistic."

As said, language evokes positive or negative connotation, but might also influence our value judgments. An illegal immigrant did something wrong – and the law should be enforced. An undocumented worker is someone who contributes to our society and just lacks some bureaucratic papers – such a worker should not be condemned.

Table 1. Terms with more positive or more negative connotations

Positive	Negative
Libertine evening	Orgy
Undocumented workers	Illegal immigrants
Family reunification	Chain migration
Critical	Cynical
Rightsizing	Downsizing
Modernizing	Reorganizing
Realistic	Fatalistic

Language encourages (or discourages) action

Language can activate people. Imagine that the leadership of an organization is making a strategic plan which includes the possibilities of a merger. Many similar organizations have already merged or consider merging, leaving the sector with less, but bigger players. A well-known frame in situations like these is that a "strategic endgame" is going on.

The "endgame" comes from the world of chess and will color the peoples perception of the situation – because it implies that the final and decisive stage of the strategic planning process has been reached. In a strategic endgame, there is no time to wait and see what happens: it is time for action. Decisions have to be made.

During the 2008 banking crisis, it becomes apparent that ABNAmro, one of Europe's systemic banks – those banks that are deemed too big to fail – is close to collapse. In the past, the bank has made a series of bad strategic decisions concerning mergers with other banks. It has made those decisions because its leaders were convinced that they were involved in a "global strategic endgame" in which any bank that did not participate in the ongoing wave of mergers would be too small to survive. In retrospect, this proved to be wrong. Pressured by the belief that this was a strategic endgame, those in charge made a number of disastrous decisions and the bank had to be saved from ruin by the government.[10]

Framing with language

If language matters, then the interesting question naturally arises: How do politicians use language to their advantage? How do they use it to convince us of the truth of their views? These questions take us into the world of political framing, which has attracted a lot of attention in recent times and forms the subject of this book.[11]

"Framing" is a phenomenon that we are already familiar with from the world of photo journalism. I could take a photo of a group of students attending my lecture. Everyone in the photo looks happy, except for three students who are looking extremely grumpy. Then what happens if I put a frame around the three grumpy students, focusing only on these three, and post the photo online along with a report about my lectures? Everyone who visits the page will see the disgruntled-looking students, and their first impression may be that the lectures were very boring and none too interesting. The frame in which something is presented influences our perception of reality.

It cannot be said that the framed photo presents an inaccurate image of the actual situation – there were indeed three grumpy students in the room. But framing does set off a process whereby we both overinterpret the reality (the three grumpy students) and underinterpret it (the other happy students). We do this not only with photos, but also with language. Table 1 presents a good example: if we call a reorganization at a company "downsizing," we overinterpreted the fact that people will be fired. We underinterpret the fact that, by doing so, the company is adapting to changing market conditions. If we call the same reorganization "right-sizing," the process of over and underinterpretation is precisely the reverse.

A frame can be defined in two ways:

- As a filter through which people perceive the world (a "communication filter" or "neural circuit")
- As the structure of a message, aimed at activating a specific interpretation of the world (a "message frame")[12]

Frames as filters

Framing can refer to a process during communication in which filters or networks in the brain help individuals interpret information. In our complex world, people categorize, classify and interpret everything they experience to make sense of the world. These processes are guided by systems of interpretation, which are referred to as primary frameworks, (communication) filters, neural circuits or frames.

In 2003, the United States and the United Kingdom declare war on Iraq. In the preceding months, a debate rages in both nations as to whether or not such an invasion should take place. On the one hand, this debate can be presented in a "Vietnam frame." From this perspective, this type of war is enormously risky; the two countries could end up in a mire of violence from which it will be very difficult to extract themselves. On the other hand, the debate can also be presented in a "Chamberlain frame" – Neville Chamberlain was the British prime minister who severely underestimated Hitler during the 1930s. Those who view the war through the filter of a Vietnam frame are obviously open to very different information than those who view it through a Chamberlain frame.

Suppose an analysts tells us that one of the risks of a war is that Iraq divides into factions that begin fighting each other? For those who filter information through the Vietnam frame, this instantly raises a red flag. A divided country has the connotation of a Vietnams-like swamp. Whereas those who espouse the Chamberlain perspective will quickly brush over this information – they see Iraq as an aggressor that seeks to attack other nations. They may feel that the possibility of Iraq dividing into competing factions might be a positive development: it would mean that Iraq could no longer be aggressive toward other countries.

Message frames

Framing can also refer to the way in which the message itself is structured. This is usually referred to as "message framing." People "frame" messages in order to emphasize a specific interpretation of the world and play down competing interpretations.[13] Message framing is about choosing the words, phrases and metaphors that invoke a specific interpretation of the world. The language that politicians use thus colors our perception of an issue: predator vs. virus, compromise vs. finding common ground, rightsizing vs. downsizing, Vietnam vs. Chamberlain. This might also be called "emphasis framing" – the process of over- and underemphasizing certain aspects of reality.[14]

In many cases, these two definitions overlap. Take the example concerning the fictional city of Addison, which deals with both the filtering and structure of messages. In this example, crime was "framed" as either a predator or a virus (message framing), but was also aimed at creating or activating internal frames that elicited different responses (frames as filters). Definitions not only overlap, there is also a process of mutual adaptation. Message framing can have an impact on people's filters. When politicians constantly employ a specific message frame (e.g., Europe is undergoing a process of Islamization), that frame may eventually become a filter that guides the audience's interpretation of the world. Likewise, politicians who know the dominant filters of their audience, may adapt their message, and make it compatible with these filters.

Structure of the book

This book examines the use of so-called "message frames" in the world of politics and policy.[15] Chapter 2 examines the characteristics and potential impact of message frames and clears up various misconceptions, such as the idea that conservative politicians are better framers than liberal politicians.

When politicians frame an issue in a certain way, their opponents will often try to reframe the debate. This game of framing and reframing is explored in Chapters 3-8. Each chapter presents a framing strategy and then discusses the most effective way to reframe the debate. Chapter 9 has a short reflection on framing: is framing morally right or wrong? It is an important question because framing is more than just spinning. Spinning has the connotation of propaganda, of biased interpretations. In Chapters 3-8 I will make clear that the game of framing and reframing can be conducive to the quality of political debates and decision-making – but there are more answers to the moral question about framing.

Framing is obviously not a new phenomenon, nor is it the preserve of right-wing politicians, as is sometimes suggested. I will therefore discuss both old and new examples of framing, as well as various left- and right-wing frames. The examples presented in this book have been carefully selected, in the hope that they will not only help you understand the game of framing and reframing but also show you how much impact you can have by using the right words.

2. What is framing and how does it work?

Electrosmog

Whenever new power lines are being installed, local residents often object on the grounds that they generate harmful electromagnetic fields. An electromagnetic field is a physical field produced by electrically charged objects. This is not an easy concept to explain to a layman, but there is another way of describing electromagnetic fields – power lines generate "electrosmog".

"Smog" has a wide range of negative associations. It is a form of air pollution that is hazardous to one's health. It is visible, grimy and can blanket an entire city. There are levels that may not be exceeded, and these can be so dangerous that smog alerts are issued. Governments sometimes take drastic action to reduce the amount of smog. The electrosmog frame, however, also obscures an important fact. Nobody disputes that smog is a health hazard, but the negative health effects of electromagnetic fields are far less clear and may not even exist. This much is clear: anybody involved in the business of installing power lines who is forced to discuss the issue with local residents in the context of this electrosmog frame is immediately put on the defensive.

This example raises several questions. What makes frames like "electrosmog" powerful? What impact does this frame have? What can you do when your opponent has such a powerful frame? These questions are enough to trigger a wider examination of framing in this chapter.[1]

What are the features of a good frame?

Frames come in all shapes and sizes. A frame can take the form of an analogy, a comparison, a metaphor, a story or simply a well-chosen phrase, one-liner or sound-bite. What are the features of a good frame?

Frames are catchy

Conservative politicians often object to development aid on the grounds that it distorts markets, disempowers people, protects corrupt regimes, and increases donor dependence. What is the essence of these arguments? How can they summarize this complex set of arguments? This is the frame that is frequently used in the debate on development aid:

> Don't give poor people fish;
> teach them how to fish.
> or
> Don't give poor people fish;
> give them fishing rods.[2]

The frame is a condensed version of the well-known Chinese proverb: "Give a man a fish and he'll eat for a day. Teach him how to fish and he'll eat for a lifetime."

It will be clear: this frame is "catchy" – it stays with you – because it conveys such a simple and convincing message. Everybody understands that teaching people to use a fishing rod is much more effective than giving them a continuous supply of fish. Catchy frames both attract attention and are easy to retain.[3] These two qualities can allow the owners of the frame to dominate the debate and make life difficult for their opponents.

We intuitively agree with frames

The second feature of a good frame is that most listeners will agree with it almost immediately. We find it hard to imagine that there are politicians who would prefer to hand out fish and prevent poor people from learning to use fishing rods.

Many right-wing parties place the fight against crime high on their agenda, and security is often a key issue during elections. The frame is often that these parties are "tough on crime."

"Tough on crime" is a catchy message. But there is more: is anybody actually against being tough on crime? Obviously not. Most people will intuitively agree with this frame – of course, you should be tough on crime.

During his second term as US president, Barack Obama argued for an economy in which everybody receives his or her "fair share."

Again, "fair share" is catchy and again, most people intuitively agree with this frame: of course, nobody deserves an unfair share. Intuitively right frames put your opponents on the defensive. If you claim to be tough on crime, the implication is that they are not. Otherwise, why would you need to point it out in the first place? If you propose a fair share, the implication is that your opponents have unfair policies.

Frames contain a villain

The fishing rod frame is catchy, people intuitively agree with this message, so the next question is: Who on earth wants to keep on handing out fish? Who doesn't want to be tough on crime? Who is in favor of an unfair share? This brings us to the third feature of frames. All good frames contain a villain – somebody who refuses to do the right thing or simply doesn't know how to. The "teach them how to fish" frame clearly points a finger at politicians on the liberal side of the political spectrum. President Obama wants a "fair share" for all and argues that "it's time to give America a raise." It carries a clear implication: "The president's political opponents don't think America deserves a raise. They are the mean, greedy bosses. Back to work, Mr. Cratchit."[4]

A good frame often set in motion a train of thought.[5] Frames are catchy, they are intuitively right and therefore there must be a villain, who hampers the right policies.

Frames challenge your opponent's core values

When you have a good frame, your opponents should think twice before stepping into it. This is because they will be forced to discuss the issue on your terms if they do. Unfortunately for them, a good frame might have another important feature: it is constructed in such a way that opponents are practically forced to step into it, because it challenges their core values.

Take the following example. In many European countries, universities charge low tuition fees and students receive government-funded maintenance grants. These low fees and government grants enable young people to go to university without incurring significant debt, which helps attract students from less affluent backgrounds. Left-wing parties generally emphasize the latter aspect, arguing that this system makes a university education available to all – not just to the children of rich parents.

But there is also another way of looking at this issue. Graduates generally go on to earn much more than nongraduates, so government funding of higher education is particularly unfair to those who don't go to college. Most European universities are already funded through taxation. Should taxpayers really be forced to cover the cost of maintenance grants as well? No, say some politicians, it is entirely reasonable to expect students to take out loans to cover their living expenses instead of receiving government grants. They frame this position with the help of a simple rhetorical question:

> Why should a baker's assistant
> pay for a future lawyer?[6]

This question has all the hallmarks of a good frame: it is "catchy" and many people will intuitively agree with it – people who work hard for little pay should not be expected to pay for someone else to go to college, who will later earn much, much more than the baker's assistant. That would be very unfair. But there is more. This frame challenges the core values of the Left, which claims to champion the less well-off – like the baker's assistant. No, says this frame, the Left actually supports those who will go on to earn a lot of money – like the future lawyer. The "baker vs. lawyer" frame thus implies that the Left has abandoned one of its core values and that this value is actually safer in the hands of its political opponents, who protect the baker's assistant by insisting that the lawyer should pay for his own studies. Experienced left-wing politicians would dismiss this frame as nonsense and present arguments to back this up. However, the point is that the attack on their core values almost forces them to step into this frame, thus putting them on the defensive.

Here is another example. Values such as individualism (people are responsible for their own actions and should never be written off collectively) and multiculturalism (it is important to treat people from other cultures with respect) are very important to certain political parties. In contrast, anti-Islamic parties in northwestern Europe like to state that immigrants from Muslim countries are causing lots of problems but that many politicians choose to look the other way. They also like to push their opponents' buttons by referring to young Muslims of North African descent as "thugs, terrorizing our streets, Islamic colonisers."[7]

These attacks on the core values of individualism and multiculturalism may anger the supporters of these values so much that they step right into these frames. They might argue that you cannot condemn an entire community for the actions of a few of its members. Or they might proclaim that many young Muslims are well integrated in Western society and that it is wrong to lump them all together. Such responses often play directly into the hands of the anti-Islamic parties, who can go on to claim that their opponents are clearly unwilling to face up to the reality of the problem.

Frames tap into social undercurrents

Every society has its undercurrents – widely held views that are more or less taken for granted. In many Western countries, people have a strong dislike of bureaucracy and overmanagement in professional organizations like schools, hospitals and the police. The common view is that there are too many managers and bureaucrats – pen pushers and box tickers – who only make things difficult for the real professionals. This is an undercurrent, a feeling of discontent shared by many people. A good frame exploits those undercurrents. Suppose, for example, that two hospitals decide to merge. This is what an opponent of the merger might say: "A bigger hospital means more managers and less health professionals, more bureaucracy and less care."

This message taps into this undercurrent. By framing your message in this language, you make it more likely that it will "stick." Many people are strongly opposed to overmanagement and bureaucracy in the public sector, they have seen it in the world of education, policing, the justice. If a frame reflects this undercurrent, people will be more inclined to condemn it. It evokes a feeling of here we go again: more managers, more bureaucrats – also in the world of health care.

Most societies are characterized by a certain amount of mistrust toward career politicians, in "Washington," "Berlin" or "Westminster" – an undercurrent that is sometimes calm and sometimes turbulent, but it is always there. In 2010, the German Federal Assembly needs to elect a new German president. The candidate of the governing coalition is Christian Wulff. His opponent is Joachim Gauck. The opposition parties frame Gauck's candidacy as follows: "Joachim Gauck brings a whole life to his candidacy; the coalition's candidate brings only a political career."[8] Joachim Gauck has real-life experience, but Christian Wulff only has a career in politics. The frame taps into an undercurrent of mistrust toward career politicians. The choice is framed as one between a man with a rich and varied life and a politician who has spent his entire life in the political fishbowl.

Of course, not all frames will have these five characteristics. But the more of these features they have, the more powerful they will be.

How does a good frame work?

As already noted, a good frame practically forces your opponent to discuss an issue on your terms. What effect does this have? What happens when one person steps into another person's frame?

Frames put opponents on the defensive

The stronger the frame, the more its opponents are put on the defensive. When people intuitively agree with a frame, the implication is that anyone who opposes it is firmly in the wrong – like those who insist on giving poor people fish rather than fishing rods. Consider the following example.

Many countries carry out national school tests in primary and secondary education. Such tests help the authorities to quantify the performance of all pupils. Should the government make these tests compulsory? And should schools be required to publish test scores so that they can be ranked? No, say many politicians. Such tests reveal very little, are far more biased than is usually claimed and cannot deal with the great differences that may exist between pupils. Moreover, publishing test scores will result in school rankings. In practice, such rankings are largely meaningless, but there is a risk that parents will focus on them to the exclusion of everything else when choosing schools for their children.

Now suppose that a certain politician is in favor of compulsory tests and school rankings. In order to frame this position in a more attractive way, the politician could say:

> Parents have a right to know
> how well schools are doing.
> After eight years of education,
> parents have a right to an objective assessment
> of where their child stands.[9]

This way of framing turns a large and complex debate about the merits of tests and rankings into a debate about a right to information. Most people would intuitively agree that such a right exists. This puts the opponents of tests on the defensive – they are trying to strip parents and students of their rights. Once they have been put in this position, it can be very hard for them to find a way out.

Frames easily get free airtime

Suppose that a minister for development cooperation becomes involved in a debate with a right-wing opponent who keeps using the "teach them how to fish" frame. Now imagine that this minister responds to his opponent's arguments in the following manner:

> I am really annoyed by this cheap rhetoric. My policy has always been to empower people, to teach them how to fish. Development aid is all about handing out fishing rods. The essence of my policy is to teach people how to fish.

This response may win over various observers, but the minister is still taking a big risk by stepping into the opponent's frame. This is because the minister is using the language – the words and images – of the opponent. Language is not a neutral vehicle for conveying information: it is loaded with value. If you use your opponents' language, you give their frame free airtime. Suppose we had watched this debate on television. What would we remember about it a few days later? Probably it will be the message that, instead of giving poor people fish, you should teach them how to fish. In other words, the minister will have actually helped to spread the opponent's message. According to American linguist George Lakoff, you should therefore never step into someone else's frame. "Do not use their language," he warns the Democrats about the Republicans. "The words draw you into their worldview."[10]

Frames place a heavy burden of proof on opponents (and a light one on their owners)

Imagine that we – the audience – have been convinced that the "teach them how to fish" frame makes sense and that we therefore have serious doubts about the impact of development aid. Put differently, a message frame has developed into a filter. This will have a strong impact on the division of the burden of proof in the debate. Suppose that a politician who opposes development aid presents two reports describing failed development projects. There may be 98 reports on other projects that prove that these other projects have been successful. However, we are observing the debate through the "teach them how to fish" frame, and are therefore very critical over development aid. Our conclusion might be that these two reports again show us that there is something fundamentally wrong with development aid. Our politician needs only two reports out of hundred to convince us.

The general mechanism is that when a frame or filter has been set, we are very receptive to information confirming that frame. As a consequence, the owners of a frame often have a light burden of proof and their opponents have a heavier burden of proof.

Frames evoke domino responses

Frames are almost always simple and a simple frame often requires a complicated response. Consider the following example. A transport authority has built a new tunnel that is experiencing many accidents and traffic jams. The authority's chief engineer is asked to explain why there are so many problems with the tunnel. The opponent is a politician who has criticized the highways authority for many years.

The discussion between the two of them unfolds as follows.

> *Chief engineer*: The tunnel employs new road markings that apparently confuse some drivers. We're also going to see if we can do anything about the lighting in the tunnel. Drivers

are telling us that the tunnel is too dark at certain points, especially in the two places where it curves slightly.

Politician: Look, of course we have to talk about road markings and lighting and curves. But there is a more fundamental problem here. The transport authority no longer has the expertise to build this type of tunnel. You are not smart enough. There are too many managers and not enough engineers. Your managers have made your organization "lean and mean." As a result, you have lost all your expertise. And if you don't have the expertise, things go wrong.

Chief engineer: We do not lack expertise. We have more than a hundred senior engineers working for us. We invest a great deal of time and effort in our people's professional development. And we make sure we keep up with the latest innovations. All our work processes are certified.

Politician: Again, there are too many managers and not enough engineers. I understand that you are investing heavily in professional development, because there is a lack of expertise within your organization. When there is a lack of expertise, things inevitably go wrong.

The "not smart enough" and "too many managers, not enough engineers" frames are catchy, attack the highway authority's core values (expertise and professional development), and tap into the undercurrent that holds that many public and private institutions are overmanaged. In this discussion, the chief engineer steps into the politician's frame and presents some impressive arguments. However, because the chief engineer puts forward four arguments, the politician has four possible ways to respond. The politician focuses on the weakest of the four arguments and builds on it. It is a well-known mechanism: a simple frame evokes a complicated response and complicated responses are almost always vulnerable. The engineer's response is what I call a domino response – the rebuttal is like a row of dominoes. If you knock over one domino, the rest will follow.

Frames are confirmed by denying them

American linguist George Lakoff frequently refers to a mechanism that is as powerful as it is simple: "When we negate a frame, we evoke the frame."[11] In 2010, Christine O'Donnell was an inexperienced Republican candidate in the Delaware Senate race. In response to accusations that she had dabbled in witchcraft in the past, she said: "I am not a witch."[12]

What sticks out in this response? The word "witch," which we will associate with her – something she probably wanted to prevent with her statement. The most famous example here is Richard Nixon's "I am not a crook," which he said when the stories about Watergate emerged. When there is smoke, there is fire. When a president feels obliged to deny that he is a crook, many people will wonder why he said that and will regard it as a confirmation instead.

In 2014, Manuel Valls, the French prime minister, visits the German chancellor to discuss the state of the European economy. He makes the following statement: "France is not the sick child of Europe."[13] Even if you are not familiar with economic issues, you start to wonder why the French prime minister would say such a thing. Why would he emphasize that France is not the sick child of Europe? Again, there's no smoke without fire. Perhaps he knows in his heart that France really is in poor health?

Many politicians in the northern parts of Europe have the opinion that France is the sick child of Europe: low economic growth, an inability to control its budget deficit. By denying this frame, the prime minster actually confirms it by reminding us that there is something wrong in the first place. We end up associating France with "sick child," just like we associate O'Donnell with "witch" and Nixon with "crook."

Reframing

Framing is a highly effective strategy, because it is hard to avoid stepping into a sophisticated frame – and anyone who does so is immediately at a disadvantage. So what to do, when confronted with a frame?

> 1. Never step into someone else's frame.
> 2. Try to reframe the debate by changing the language that is being used to discuss the issue.

The next chapters have a detailed overview of strategies in this game of framing and reframing. For now, two very simple examples of how this game is played.

In 2016, Donald Trump loses the primaries in Iowa. The main reason is that his campaign staff does not understand well enough how the caucus system works and how the "ground game" is played in Iowa. He is simply unaware of some fundamental mechanisms in the world of campaigning. But how does he frame these?

> Don't forget, Joe,
> I'm doing this for the first time.
> I'm like a rookie
> and I'm learning fast
> and I do learn fast,
> and I think we're doing really great.[14]

Being inexpert, not having the expertise to run a campaign, is reframed as "learning fast" – which, of course, has a very positive connotation.

Another example: in 2017, Donald Trump has a conversation with Sergey Lavrov, the Russian minister of foreign affairs. During this conversation, Trump reveals highly classified information to Lavrov, about IS terrorism.[15] This information came from an ally of the US that did not give permission to inform the Russians. The frames: "a major breach of espionage etiquette," "angering a partner," "calling into question the ability of the United States to keep secrets," and a White House that is out of control.[16] How does Trump reframe the debate? Like the US, the Russians are fighting IS and this was all about

> information sharing,
> collaboration,
> and airline flight safety.[17]

"Revealing highly classified information" has a negative connotation and is reframed as "information sharing" with a partner the US collaborates with – reframes that have a positive connotation.

What is the underlying strategy here? It is very simple: a negative qualification (e.g., inexpert) is replaced by a positive qualification (e.g., learning fast). When you are faced with a negative frame, google a bit on "antonyms of ..." and you will find words that emphasize something positive. So the essence of reframing is:

- Do not step into your opponent's frame by using their terms, such as by talking about "inexpert" or "revealing classified information."
- Instead, reframe the debate and use language that strengthens your position, such as by talking about "learning fast" or "information sharing."
- Force your opponents to step into your new frame. If they criticize you being inexpert, say they apparently don't see that people have development potential, that people learn. If they criticize you for revealing information, say you are working on airline flight safety with one of your allies. What's wrong with that?

Again, these are very simple examples of the game of framing and reframing. In this game, politicians use more sophisticated strategies – consciously or unconsciously – and these strategies result in recurrent patterns in this game. In the next chapters, these strategies and patterns will be discussed – but first there are two important questions that have to be answered.

Is reframing just another word for side-stepping debate?

Many people are irritated by the fact that politicians often refuse to answer questions. They evade journalists' queries in interviews and fail to respond to their opponent's arguments in debates. From this perspective, reframing might be seen as not answering questions or not responding to arguments – and focusing on your own narrative instead. Surely this is precisely the kind of behavior that people find so annoying in politicians.

Is reframing just another word for side-stepping the debate? In order to answer this question, here is an analysis of a typical exchange between two politicians: a European anti-Muslim populist (the well-known Dutch politician Geert Wilders) and a social democrat (former leader of the Dutch Partij van de Arbeid [Labor Party] and former mayor of Amsterdam Job Cohen):

> *Geert Wilders*: Mass immigration and Islamization is costing us €7.2 billion a year, and you strongly support it. [...] You have driven hundreds of local residents out of Amsterdam by drinking tea with dodgy imams while those residents were being harassed by Moroccan delinquents. What we need is leadership, an end to immigration and law and order, not somebody who has a cup of tea with a dodgy imam when things start to get tough.
> *Job Cohen*: I agree with you entirely that we need leadership. And what I have done in Amsterdam in recent years is to refuse to distinguish between people based on their differences. As far as I'm concerned, freedom of religion means freedom of religion for all. And then it doesn't matter where you come from or what your background is, the only thing that matters is what you intend to do now that you're here. Those who are engaged in worthwhile pursuits will be encouraged, and those who cause trouble will be dealt with accordingly.[18]

This exchange can be interpreted in several ways. The first interpretation is a negative one: there is no real debate here, since Cohen does not respond to Wilders's arguments. We therefore see two politicians talking at cross-purposes, which is precisely what politicians are famous for doing.

There is a second interpretation: Cohen deliberately avoids stepping into Wilders's anti-Muslim frame, thus ensuring that he does not have to conduct the debate on Wilders's terms. If he were to step into Wilders's frame, he would have to defend himself against the accusation that he has driven hundreds of former residents out of Amsterdam and that he mixes with radical Muslim clerics. That would be a very risky strategy, because the whole debate would then focus on those issues.

The third interpretation is much more positive: Cohen has not stepped into Wilders's anti-Muslim frame and as a consequence of that, the debate reveals the essence of their political differences. For Wilders, the key issues are immigration, Islamization and law and order. For Cohen, what matters is equal treatment and respect. Because neither of them are willing to abandon their key messages, the differences between them become crystal clear – there is a free and open battle of ideas.

The message here: any one of these three interpretations may be correct and therefore the idea that reframing is just another word for politicians side-stepping debate is overly simplistic.

Is the Right better at framing than the Left?

The idea that the Right is better at framing than the Left was strongly nourished by George Lakoff, the American linguist who first introduced the concept of framing to a wider audience in 2004. One of the key questions in his book *Don't Think of an Elephant* is why Republicans so often manage to win their debates against Democrats. His answer is that the Republicans are good at framing and that they know how to choose the right words. The Democrats constantly allow themselves to be sucked into Republican frames and require overly complicated intellectual arguments to explain their own positions.[19] In *The Sound Bite Society*, Jeffrey Scheuer makes a similar point. He notes that television has created a sound-bite culture and that the simplicity inherent in sound-bites has become a core value of the conservative political message.[20] In contrast, the liberal Left in the United States has a complex message – and the sound-bite culture punishes them for this. Why is the liberal message more complex than the conservative message, according to many liberal politicians? Because those on the Left want to change the world, while those on the Right want to keep things as they are. Because left-wing politicians focus on bigger-than-self issues, while right-wing politicians focus mainly on self issues. Because people who advocate change will always encounter more challenges than those who want to maintain the status quo.

However, conservatives see things very differently. According to Arthur C. Brooks, a member of a conservative think tank, liberal frames portray conservatives as rigid, heartless and unconcerned about ordinary people. When Obama uses his "fair share" frame that claims "It's time to give Americans a raise," he implies that his opponents are opposed to this idea. This type of frame is constantly used to demonize the Right – at least, according to Brooks, as if all it cares about is helping the rich and harming the poor. In fact, conservative policies such as deregulation and lowering taxes increase the prosperity of Americans. Moreover, according to a US study, conservative households donate on average 30 percent more to charity than liberal households, despite earning 6 percent less.[21]

Why is the conservative narrative so much harder to frame than the liberal narrative, according to many conservative politicians? Those on the Left have it relatively easy, because they focus on the day-to-day concerns of real people, while those on the Right look at the bigger picture, such as how to stimulate the economy in order to create more jobs. The same applies to the refugee issue. Liberals focus on the care of individual refugees, while conservatives are left to deal with the difficult issue of reducing the flow of refugees.

It is up to you to decide what you make of these competing claims. What is clear, however, is that both the Left and the Right complain about the other side's superficial framing and the disadvantages of their own complex narrative. It would thus seem that we are perhaps inclined to believe that others are using frames while we are simply trying to convey a message that is real, honest and complex.

Part Two

Strategies

3. The 3P model

Sarah Palin about policy: "Does that really mean anything?"

Sarah Palin – former governor of Alaska and Republican vice presidential candidate in 2008 – once complimented an opponent after a debate. She was deeply impressed by his expertise and knowledge of the relevant facts and policies, but added:

> But then I look over the crowd
> and wonder,
> does that really mean anything?[1]

In Palin's experience, people don't care very much about policy. We come across this idea in other places, too. Political communication is all about "fighting for people rather than against policies," says a political analyst.[2] "I'm going to have to show my heart, show who I am, tell my story," says a presidential candidate.[3] How does an experienced politician tackle voter cynicism? Bill Clinton has an advice to the people of Virginia: "You need to turn the light on in Virginia and let the light shine and let people feel the future flowing through their veins, in their hearts, in their minds, and their spirits."[4]

Three Ps

"Feel the future flowing" – this is not a dry policy statement, this is an emotion. It brings us to the first structure in the game of framing and reframing: the 3P model. Politicians who want to obtain support for their message have three basic options. They can do one of the following:

- Bring their *policy* to the attention of the public
- Focus on the underlying *principles*, or
- Highlight a *personal experience* with the issue

Frames can be about policy, underlying principles or personal experiences (of politicians themselves or of other people). These three options together make up the 3P model which can be used to understand the game of framing and reframing.

Policy

Policy frames are about objectives, about the analysis of the problem that will be solved, about measures that will be taken. They are about the implementation of these measures, the costs and the intended effects. Policy frames are accordingly all about facts and figures – they are very analytical.

This is an example of a policy frame:

> I want to increase small business tax deductions by 25 percent, and I will tell you why. This country has a problem: it is not attractive enough for entrepreneurial people. The total number of entrepreneurs has not gone up in the past four years. Increasing small business tax deductions by 25 percent, will create strong financial incentives for people to start new businesses. An entrepreneur with a turnover of 250,000 will receive a net income rise of 2,500.

What is the risk of a policy statement like this? Policy is always complex and this statement therefore immediately raises several questions. Why 25 percent and not 15 or 35? What type of activity is covered by the small business tax? Why increase deductions for this tax but not others? What impact will the deductions have on business, employment, and the national deficit? It is clear that a discussion that focuses solely on policy quickly runs a risk of getting bogged down in definitions, facts and figures, and competing analyses.

A policy frame conveys information, but this information is often complex and open to different interpretations. In fact, many policy proposals can only be understood by people with expert knowledge of the issue concerned. And tax deductions are just one issue. Who can possibly get a handle on the entire policy portfolio – and all the ideas – espoused by a single politician or party?

Principle

Now let's look at the same policy presented in a principle frame:

> I want to increase small business tax deductions by 25 percent, and I will tell you why. Entrepreneurs are hard-working people. They create jobs. They take risks. They bring innovations to this country. They want to create something new. They want to take control of their future. They don't want to depend on other people.

These are the words of a politician who is extolling principles or values such as risk-taking, self-reliance, ingenuity, and job creation. There are two key differences between principles and policy frames. First, principles affect our deeply held convictions and emotions. The principles in this example include a belief in the value of hard work, risk-taking and the freedom to shape one's own destiny. Anyone who shares these principles is likely to be affected by them.

When politicians successfully refer to values, we agree with, they become "one of us." Even if you don't fully understand the policy they are proposing, you believe that they will always defend your values and interests. When politicians tell us about their policies, they are primarily conveying information. When they refer to principles we share, they establish a relationship with us, which is probably more important than the details of the policy in question.

George W. Bush is a Republican who was able to count on the support of almost 50 percent of all Hispanic voters when he ran for president – something that is rather extraordinary for a conservative politician. How did he manage that? As a former governor of Texas, he explained his view on immigration: "Family values don't stop at the Rio Grande and a hungry mother is going to try to feed her child."[5]

Family values are a core principle of Republican ideology. Bush extended this principle to a mother crossing the Rio Grande in search of a better future for her child. According to a Republican analyst: "When Hispanics heard that, they knew he cared and were willing to listen to his policies on education, jobs, spending, etc. Because his first sentence struck a chord, Hispanic Americans were willing to listen to his second sentence."[6] Principles create a relationship, strike a chord.

The second key difference between principles and policy is that all political parties adopt hundreds of different policy positions, which is too much for one person to comprehend. In contrast, most political parties only advocate a limited number of core principles, which are much easier to grasp. As the world becomes more complex and politicians are required to adopt an increasing number of positions, the more important these core principles become.

Principle frames can be persuasive – even so persuasive that they enable politicians to secure the support of voters whose interests are actually harmed by the policies they are proposing. How is it possible, investigative journalist Thomas Frank asks, that poor people in Kansas defected en masse from the Democrats to the Republicans, who subsequently stripped away the welfare system on which they depended? What motivates voters to act against their own interests? Frank discovered that the Democrats campaigned on the basis of their policies and that the Republicans campaigned on the basis of their values, which clearly exercised a much stronger appeal.[7] Arlie Russell Hochschild found something similar in Louisiana: Louisiana has a high level of industrial pollution, but many Louisianians are against environmental regulations. Why? Because regulations come from the federal government – and the federal government cannot be trusted,[8] which makes anti-big government rhetoric very effective.

Personal experience

There is yet another way to defend the tax deductions:

> I want to increase small business tax deductions by 25 percent and I will tell you why. I come from a family of entrepreneurs, and I know how hard my parents used to work. I saw how difficult it was for them when things didn't go well with the business for a couple of years. I can also remember how proud they were when things picked up again and they were able to expand the business.

Policy frames convey information, while principle frames are about establishing a relationship with the public on the basis of shared values. Politicians who express a personal experience – their own experience or the experience of somebody else – also enter into a relationship with their audience, in this case by convincing entrepreneurs that they are just like them or by giving a policy a human face. The impact of this: we are more easily willing to give them a license to operate and make policy on our behalf. Maybe the most iconic example of personal engagement is Bill Clinton's response to Bob Rafsky, an AIDS sufferer and activist. Rafsky accused Clinton:

> We're not dying of AIDS
> as much as we are dying
> of eleven years of government neglect.

Clinton's response is very personal:

> I feel your pain.[9]

Rafsky criticizes the Clinton's policies, but Clinton does not respond by talking policy. He responds by expressing his personal feelings. Policies are cold, feelings are warm. Policies are about conveying information, personal experiences create a relationship – not only between Clinton and Rafsky, but also between Clinton and people sympathizing with Rafsky.

Figure 1.   The 3P model: Three types of frames

Figure 1 provides a representation of the 3P model.[10] Policy frames are about conveying information, which is generally a "cold" activity. In contrast, principle frames and personal experience frames are about establishing a relationship with the audience, which is a "warm" activity. The three Ps are, of course, interconnected, policy only becomes meaningful when it is linked to certain principles or when it is given a human face. When people are moved by politicians' values or feel a personal connection with them, they become more receptive to their policies.

How to reframe with the 3P model?

How is the 3P model used in the game of framing and reframing? The essence is very simple:

- If you are confronted with a frame based on one of the three Ps, don't enter into your opponent's frame.
- Instead, reframe the issue using one or both of the other Ps.

A policy frame can be countered with principles or a personal experience. A principle frame can be undermined by talking about policies or personal experiences. Finally, a personal experience frame can be challenged through policies or principles. Here are the examples.

Figure 2.   Reframing and the 3P model

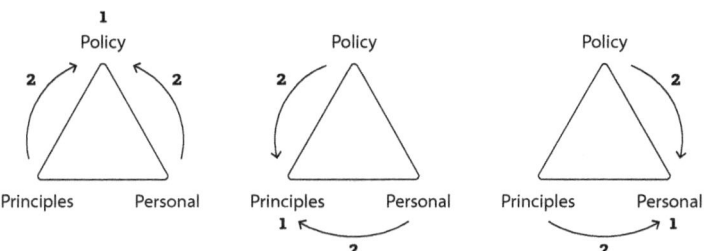

Reframing through principles

Ronald Reagan: "Why is it inflationary?"
During the 1980 US presidential election campaign, President Jimmy Carter and his challenger, Ronald Reagan, take part in a debate. Reagan, who is the ultimate representative of the Republican party's core principles of individual freedom and distrust of big government, proposes substantial tax cuts. Carter opposes these cuts and put forward a very analytical policy frame arguing that they will cause inflation. Carter's frame is potentially very powerful for two reasons:

- Many Americans are deeply concerned about inflation, which has reached double digits by 1979.
- Reagan's plan threatens to reduce the value of the savings of hard-working Americans. There are core values at stake here.

Carter's frame puts Reagan in a lose-lose situation: he could either withdraw his proposed tax cuts (and lose the debate) or accept responsibility for increasing inflation (and also lose the debate). However, instead of stepping into Carter's policy frame, Reagan responds by reframing the debate with help of his principles. Regarding the idea that his tax-cut proposal is inflationary, Reagan says:

> I would like to ask the president
> why is it inflationary
> to let the people keep more of their money
> and spend it the way that they like,
> and it isn't inflationary
> to let him take that money
> and spend it the way he wants?[11]

Reagan does not address Carter's allegation that cutting taxes would cause inflation. Instead, he refers to key Americans values: less tax means less government and therefore more individual freedom – a value that is deeply rooted in American culture. Tax cuts are consistent with the American ethos and the ideals of the Founding Fathers. Reagan thus reframes the debate by shifting the focus from policy (his proposal is inflationary) to principles (taxes are un-American).

This strategy has several advantages. First, Reagan does not have to discuss Carter's economic argument because he does not step into his policy frame. Second, by invoking time-honored American values, he makes it difficult for Carter to challenge him on this point, putting the president on the defensive. Third, values are intertwined with emotions, makings things even harder for Carter. Any discussion along these lines will quickly set his "cold and sterile" policy analysis against Reagan's "warm" values. Fourth, value frames are simple. For many people, Carter's policy frame is rather complicated. Who understands the connection between tax cuts and inflation? How can something so positive (tax cuts) have any negative consequences (inflation)? In contrast, the values that Reagan invokes are easy to understand. In fact, the idea that the government should stay out of people's lives as much as possible has not changed since the American Revolution.

An obvious disadvantage of Reagan's response is that it may be regarded as shallow and irrelevant. A close reading of the debate reveals that Reagan presents some figures and analysis – thus demonstrating that he isn't economically illiterate – but thanks to his focus on values he still faces a much lower burden of proof. According to William Lewis, who studied Reagan's use of rhetoric, "If the move from practicality to principle is accepted, it makes the policy immune from most objections."[12]

Reframing through personal experiences

George W. Bush: "I'm the kind of person …"
In a debate between Al Gore and George W. Bush during the 2000 US presidential election campaign, the discussion turns to equal treatment of homosexuals. At the time, there is a bill before Congress that will make it unlawful to fire homosexual people based solely on their sexual orientation. Gore asks Bush whether he would support the bill.

This policy-related question places Bush in a lose-lose frame, just like Carter did to Reagan in the debate about tax cuts. If Bush were to say "yes," he would get into trouble with large sections of his party, who regard equal treatment as special treatment. On the other hand, a "no" would confirm the image of Bush that Gore wanted to depict, namely a person who would ultimately not support equal rights for gays and lesbians. Moreover, any answer that falls between a straightforward "yes" or "no" risks irritating both Bush's supporters and the supporters of the bill. In the event, Bush responds as follows:

> I will tell you
> I'm the kind of person,
> I don't hire or fire somebody
> based upon their sexual orientation.
> As a matter of fact,
> I'd like to take the issue a little farther.
> I don't really think it's any of my –
> you know, any of my concerns what –
> how you conduct your sex life.

> And I think that's a private matter.
> And I think that's the way it ought to be.
> But I'm going to be respectful for people,
> I'll tolerate people,
> and I support equal rights
> but not special rights for people.[13]

What happens here?[14] Bush does not give a "yes" or a "no" and does not step into Gore's lose-lose frame. He reframes the issue instead. He counters the policy frame by talking about his personal beliefs and attitude – he is an honest and fair person who would never discriminate against anyone. As a result, Gore suddenly finds himself in a totally different frame. How can he counter Bush's position? He can hardly challenge his personal integrity. After Bush places the issue of equal treatment in a personal engagement frame, Gore's attack fizzles out.

Marco Rubio: "You're the only person ... "
During the 2016 Republican presidential primaries, Donald Trump and Senator Marco Rubio frequently face off against each other. One of Trump's key talking points is that he wants to "bring jobs back to America." According to Trump, too many US jobs are being transferred abroad or given to illegal immigrants, who should all be deported.

This is clearly a policy frame. How does Rubio reframe the debate? He refers to Trump's exclusive Mar-a-Lago club in Palm Beach:

> We saw a report in one of the newspapers
> that Donald, you've hired
> a significant number of people
> from other countries
> to take jobs that Americans could have filled.
> My mom and dad –
> my mom was a maid at a hotel,
> and instead of hiring an American like her,

> you have brought in over a thousand people
> from all over the world
> to fill those jobs instead. [...]
> You're the only person
> on this stage
> that has ever been fined
> for hiring people
> to work on your projects illegally.[15]

Rubio is reframing the debate: from policy to Trump personally. Trump advocates a certain policy, but as a business man does the exact opposite. His reframe is, of course, very uncomfortable for Trump.

Reframing through policy

As discussed above, referring to principles and personal experiences enables politicians to establish a relationship with their audience. In contrast, policy frames are often simply about conveying information, which renders them much less powerful. However, that doesn't mean that they can't be used to reframe a debate. On the contrary.

David Cameron: "Judge us on our record"
During the 2015 UK general election campaign, Conservative prime minister David Cameron and Boris Johnson – the Conservative mayor of London – participate in a public debate in which a member of the audience asked the following question:

> Do you think the UK's current democracy-crippling voter apathy is caused by the fact that its prime minister, mayor of the capital, and chancellor were all in the same class at school, are all industriously dismantling the nation's assets and selling them off to their mates, are all related to banking families and have been proven, over and over again, to be singularly self-interested in every political decision they've ever made?

This frame focuses on Cameron's personal engagement, claiming that he is a member of a privileged elite that is out of touch with the everyday concerns of ordinary citizens. It is a deeply personal attack that questions his commitment to serving all the people of Britain.

However, instead of stepping into this personal frame, Cameron reframes the debate:

> I would say: Judge us on our record.
> Two million more people in work in our country.
> The deficit cut by half.
> An economy growing faster than the rest of the European Union.
> And frankly, a choice that we made when I became prime minister. [...]
> We said we're going to invest in our National Health Service, every single year.
> More money. [...]
> That wasn't a Lib-Dem policy,
> that wasn't a Labour policy,
> that was a David Cameron Conservative policy
> and it was the right thing to do.

Cameron reframes the question about his privileged background by referring to his successful policies. Cameron and the Conservatives should be judged on their policy record, which has been very good. After all, if everyone in Britain is better off, what does it matter if some politicians come from a privileged background?

Then Boris Johnson jumps in:

> I don't think the people of this country
> care about where you come from.
> What they care is what you're doing,
> what you're saying to the country
> and how you're going to take it forward.[16]

Johnson reframes the question about him as a person by referring to principles. It does not matter where you come from – what matters is what you contribute to society. By turning Cameron's background into an issue, the person who asked the original question has violated this important British value.

Is framing and reframing through the 3P model just a political game?

The 3P model highlights a key feature of reframing: by using the model, there is a sudden shift in perspective. Just when you think your frame places you in a strong position, someone comes along to reframe the issue and your position becomes a liability.

Is this simply political game playing? No. There is more at stake here.

Nobody can deny that policy matters, but so do principles. We are therefore entitled to question politicians about the values on which their policies are based. There are hundreds of issues on the policy agenda, and politicians make dozens of decisions every day. Those decisions become nothing more than random acts if they cannot be traced to certain key principles. Without a "master narrative" regarding those principles, we would be left with a sense that politicians have opinions on everything while not really standing for anything.[17]

Policy matters, principles matter, but there is also the question whether we can entrust people to make decisions on our behalf. A politician's level of personal experience and engagement is therefore also a relevant consideration.

In other words, if policy, principles, and personal experiences matter, it is completely legitimate to challenge politicians from all three perspectives.

When a politician advocates cutting unemployment benefits because it will financially incentivize people to seek work, it is, of course, entirely reasonable to ask whether this approach works in practice (policy). It is also reasonable to ask questions about the underlying values of this politician. For example, opponents might ask whether this policy is based on the cynical belief that people are merely money driven, and are not inclined to seek work in the absence of financial incentives (principles). Likewise, it is totally legitimate to ask politicians whether they know people who will be affected by the cuts and how they feel about the fact that some of them will have to survive on a lower monthly payment (personal experience).

The 3P model is thus not merely a debating tool that helps politicians play the game of framing and reframing. It embraces three legitimate perspectives in the world of politics.

4. Victims, villains, and heroes

The daddy tax

In a large European city, there is anger about the behavior a group of young men who have fathered children with several different women and then abandoned them. The mothers in question, who are often as young as eighteen, are left to raise these children by themselves and are living in poverty. One local politician is particularly incensed by this:

> I believe this is unacceptable.
> I believe a man should take responsibility
> for any children he fathers.
> You can't expect society to pick up the tab.
> It's perfectly reasonable
> that he should cover the cost of raising his children.[1]

It is even worse, the politician says. Some of the men are also claiming unemployment benefits. That is why he proposes a "daddy tax."

A daddy tax means, first, that the benefit payments of the fathers will be taxed 100 percent and, second, that the revenues of this tax will be transferred to the mothers.

Is this proposal feasible? Not in the slightest: there are all kinds of legal impediments – the men could simply deny paternity, and refuse DNA testing. The policy will not work. Nevertheless, the politician receives widespread praise for this proposal.

Why? What make this frame of the daddy tax powerful? Let's answer this question with help of a little thought experiment. There is a second politician who argues that this a much more complex problem than the daddy tax politician suggests. There are more structural causes for the behavior of these men, like social and economic disparities, and educational inequality. The opponent advocates an entirely different approach: the authorities should enter into a dialogue with the fathers, provide mediation and counseling and organize parenting classes.

The two politicians are thus on opposite sides of the debate. One is proposing a daddy tax, while the other is in favor of dialogue, to restore the relationship between fathers and mothers. Which approach is likely to be more popular with the public? From the outset, the daddy tax satisfies many of the requirements of a good frame. First, it is simple and catchy. Second, many people intuitively agree with chasing the fathers and protecting the mothers. Third, any politician who opposes this narrative runs the risk of being framed as someone who refuses to do what needs to be done.

Three roles

But that's not all. The actions of these young men also provoke anger and moral outrage. When people experience such strong emotions, their tolerance for complexity often decreases. As a result, they like to keep things simple: there are victims (the mothers and children) and villains (the fathers). Once we have internalized this division of roles, we start looking for someone to play the third and key role in this drama – that of the hero.[2]

The victim-villain-hero model is often used in the world of framing and reframing, in at least two ways:

- Politicians might cast their opponents as a villain, which is, of course, not a very attractive role and will put these opponents on the defensive, or
- Politicians might cast themselves as heroes, and their opponents, implicitly of explicitly, as defenders or supporters of the villain, which also puts them on the defensive.

The latter approach can be recognized in the example of the daddy tax politician. The daddy tax politician is the hero who chases the villain. Once this frame has become popular, the dialogue politician can easily become someone who defends the villain and who is therefore morally wrong.

Figure 3. The victim-villain-hero model

The emotional trigger: Negative and positive emotions

Critics will argue that this victim-villain-hero frame oversimplifies complex issues. In real life, problems usually have several causes, so there is often no clear-cut villain. Likewise, solutions may be incomplete or create new problems in other areas, so there is often no obvious hero. And what about the victims? Even they may not be as innocent as they first appear. In other words, reality is much more complicated than this frame implies.

These critics are probably right. Despite all this, the frame is an effective tool for controlling the public debate, especially when it comes to highly emotive issues. As our emotions take over, we become increasingly susceptible to the kind of simple reasoning that underlies this frame. Emotions are thus the trigger of this frame – the spark that lights the fuse. There is, of course, the question how simple frames relate to the real-world complexity – I will come back to that question in Chapter 9.

The frame can be triggered by negative emotions, such as anger, moral outrage, or pessimism. According to German philosopher Peter Sloterdijk, anger can lead to calls for firm action and a phenomenon he refers to as the "politics of impatience."[3] When a complex issue is reduced to a simple formula in which the problem, the cause, and the solution are already known, people expect politicians to act as swiftly as possible. Anyone who is deeply outraged at another person's suffering automatically looks for villains and yearns for a hero to take firm and immediate action.

The frame can also be triggered by positive emotions, such as hope, optimism, or expectation. According to British philosopher Roger Scruton, hope and optimism can lead to a simplistic belief in the power of planning to settle complex problems with simple solutions. An idealistic person who is emotionally committed to making the world a better place will quickly denounce as a villain anyone who challenges his or her goals or methods. And if there is a villain, there must also be victims who suffer in the present and look forward to a future in which they will no longer be victims. This situation calls out for a hero who will make the world a better place. Scruton refers to this attitude as "unscrupulous optimism," because it willfully ignores the complexities of the real world.[4]

Both negative and positive emotions are "comfortable certainties."[5] Outrage and optimism both make life easier – and more comfortable – by relieving us of the need to confront the complexities of modern existence.

What do we expect from a hero?

First of all, heroes must show compassion for the victims and condemn the villains. One of the strengths of the proposed "daddy tax" is that it smacks of righteous anger. In contrast, the dialogue-based solution proposed by the second politician does exactly the opposite. Why should we have dialogue with villains?

Second, we expect the hero to take action – to protect the victims and punish the villains. The "daddy tax" is a tough sanction that fits this expectation perfectly. The soft measures proposed by the second politician are, of course, not appropriate for villains.

Third, heroes who take firm action also show that they are in control of the situation. There is a clear problem (the women who are forced to raise their children single-handedly), a clear cause (the young men), and a clear solution (the "daddy tax"). The second politician's narrative is much more complicated and ambiguous. Because there are so many causes (social, economic, and educational), the problem is no longer clear-cut, and the solution even less so – our second politician seems to be out of control.

Fourth, we expect the hero not only to take action, but also to take action immediately, in the here and now. Once again, the second politician does not live up to this hope. On the contrary, dialogue, mediation, and counseling will clearly not have an immediate impact on the problem. The "daddy tax," on the other hand, is practically synonymous with an instant result. Money taken from the fathers can be given directly to the mothers.

In a slightly different version of this frame, the hero is also a victim, because the villain is targeting him, too. Populist politicians love using this version of the victim-villain-hero frame. In their narrative, the political elites are the villains, ordinary hard-working people are the victims, and the populist politician who dares challenge the villains is the hero. The hero, however, is also criticized or sidelined or even persecuted by the political elite, and is therefore a fellow-victim.

Geert Wilders: Persecuted and denied entry

Dutch anti-immigration politician Geert Wilders claims to stand up for the ordinary citizen, who is completely fed up with mass immigration – but Geert Wilders is ignored, or even despised, by the political elites:

> As you may know, I am being persecuted in my own country.
> For the past four and a half years, I have not been able to move around freely,
> and I have been forced to live in secret locations.
> The left-wing elite does not care because it is blinded by cultural relativism.

Their contempt for the West is much greater
than their appreciation of the freedoms we enjoy here.
As a result, they are willing to give up everything.
Two weeks ago I tried to enter the United Kingdom, an EU country.
I was denied entry, spent three hours in custody,
and was then put on the first available airplane back to the Netherlands.[6]

Anyone who is angry about immigration will obviously be susceptible to a frame that portrays the various protagonists as victims, villains, and heroes. Not surprisingly, he or she will become even more angry if the villain starts going after the hero, too – in this case: the left-wing elite going after Wilders.

The double bind of the villain

The power of the victim-villain-hero frame becomes clear when we consider the position of the villain versus the hero and victim.

Once a politician has been framed as a hero, there is a strong incentive for this politician to reconfirm the frame – being a hero is a very attractive role. The same goes more or less for the victim – a victim has the moral right to be supported and safeguarded, so the role of victim might be very attractive. The villain, however, is often faced with a double bind: no matter how villains respond – by denying or admitting that they are villains – the frame of being a villain will be reconfirmed. It might therefore be very difficult to escape this frame, once the roles have been attributed.

An example of this double bind comes from the health-care sector. In many countries, there is a lot of resistance to the proliferation of managers in the health-care sector. They are branded as villains because they have no medical expertise and because the procedures they introduce only create more bureaucratic hurdles and restrictions. Who are the victims? Patients who need good care and doctors who want to provide it but are prevented from doing so by red tape, bureaucracy and overmanagement.

Once there is a victim and a villain, the role of the hero becomes increasingly attractive. In this case, the hero could be a politician who is willing to take on the managers using the following language:

> We need to cut bureaucracy and red tape.
> There should be fewer administrators
> and more frontline medical staff.
> The country does not need
> useless pen-pushers and box-tickers.
> We need to cut the 6,500-strong army
> of health bureaucrats.[7]

What effect does this division of roles have on managers-villains? If they deny that the health-care sector is overmanaged, they are obviously blind to what is going on. This simply turns them into an even bigger villain. Alternatively, if they admit that there is a problem, they simply end up confirming the hero's frame. Once you have been framed as a villain, you will be faced with this double bind, which is one of the reasons why this frame is often so powerful.

The frame also makes things very easy for the victims, who don't have to think too hard or take a critical look at themselves. Fortunately for them, it turns out that there is a single scapegoat for all the problems in the health-care sector: the villain. Victims can therefore issue demands and are clearly entitled to the hero's help. Who dares to tell the victims in the health-care sector that they need to be more resilient, that they should show some initiative, or that they are partly responsible for some of the problems in the sector? You can try this, but it is a risky strategy.

Explanation + emotion = justification

The more anger a villain evokes, the less tolerant we are of politicians taking the side of a villain. Even an explanation or an analysis of the villain's behavior might be risky. In debates about crime, for example, there is the familiar reasoning that criminal behavior is a result of poor education or poverty. What is the risk of such reasoning?

The explanation is meant as an analysis – and, of course, anyone who wants to solve the problem of crime needs to analyze it. But: "It is not what you say; it is what people hear."[8] In the heat of emotion, what is meant as an explanation can be seen as a justification of crime.

Let me give an example that has a totally different historical significance to all the other examples in this book. In 1988 the president of the German Bundestag, Philipp Jenninger, gives a speech commemorating the fiftieth anniversary of Kristallnacht, the pogrom against Jews in Nazi Germany on 9-10 November 1938.

Of course Jenninger totally and unambiguously rejects Nazism. Among the issues covered in his speech, he asks the question of how the Germans could have been so blinded by Hitler. How could this have happened? Jenninger says, among other things:

> For the Germans who overwhelmingly had felt the Weimar Republic as the consequence of foreign, political humiliation, this all [the rise of Hitler] must have appeared to be a miracle. And not only that, from massive unemployment came full employment, from massive misery came a type of prosperity for most levels. Instead of desperation and hopelessness there was optimism and self-confidence.[9]

Jenninger is explaining the rise of Hitler at an intensely emotional moment: the commemoration of Kristallnacht. What is meant as an explanation is seen as a justification: many members of the Bundestag are so upset by Jenninger's speech, that they leave the meeting hall. "The CDU clings to the shadow of the past" writes *Der Spiegel*, a German news magazine.[10] Jenninger is forced to resign.

The risk of defusing the frame

A politician who has been cast as a villain might be tempted to undermine this casting by defusing its emotional trigger. This is, however, a risky strategy and a good example of the double bind the villain often has to live with. A villain who tries and fails to diffuse the emotional trigger will probably become an even bigger villain. Consider the following two examples.

Barack Obama: The people are scared

During the 2010 midterm elections, which take place in the middle of President Obama's first term in office, the Democrats suffer heavy losses. At the time, the US economy is in a very bad shape. The Republicans claim that Obama wants to seize control of the banking system, the health-care industry, and the energy sector and that his anti-business, pro-big government policies have produced a billion-dollar deficit. The narrative is clear. Obama is a villain who is trampling traditional American values. Ordinary Americans, who are wary of the government at the best of times, are the victims. The Republicans, finally, are the heroes. How does Obama respond to this narrative? He says:

> And so part of the reason
> that our politics seems so tough right now,
> and facts and science and argument
> does not seem to be winning the day all the time,
> is because we're hard-wired
> not to always think clearly
> when we're scared.
> And the country is scared,
> and they have good reason to be.[11]

In this example, Obama points the finger at the emotion of being scared. America is scared, he says, and this fear is giving rise to naïve and one-dimensional views regarding his policies.

Obama's opponents are incensed by this. "If you're unemployed, sitting in your living room, and you hear the president say that you don't understand the real problem because you're scared, you get really, really angry," explains a Republican strategist.

This is the lesson: when someone doesn't respect our emotions – our anger, our optimism, our desires – we feel personally attacked. Also, our emotions are connected to our hopes and values – the things that make us who we are. Defusing an emotional frame is therefore a dangerous strategy: when Obama says America is scared, he takes the risk of confirming the frame instead of defusing it. By dismissing the victims' fears and refusing to acknowledge their legitimate concerns, he becomes an even greater villain. In the meantime, the Republicans are still the heroes.

Jealousy tax

The second example relates to the widespread moral outrage over inflated salaries and bonuses in certain parts of the private sector. In many countries, the gap between the rich and the poor is widening. Corporate salaries, which are already very high, are rising much faster than the wages of middle- and low-income earners. A person who is morally outraged over this will regard any politician who proposes higher taxes for high-income individuals as a hero. The victims in this scenario are the middle- and low-income earners. The villains are the high earners, the recipients of massive bonuses, and anyone who is opposed to raising taxes for high-income individuals.

Opponents of higher taxes describe these as "jealousy taxes."

This is a clear attempt to defuse an emotional frame by substituting a positive – or at least a defensible – emotion (moral outrage) with a negative one (jealousy). This again is a risky strategy, because any politician who uses it may be accused of having contempt for other people's moral concerns. Politicians who are already regarded as villains because they are opposed to raising taxes for high-income individuals will thus be regarded as even greater villains if they dismiss moral outrage on this issue as plain old envy.

How to reframe?

Let's return to the daddy tax and the dialogue politician. This dialogue-politician has been casted as the villain. Does this mean that the dialogue politician will always lose a debate like this? No – if this politician also manages to fuel an emotion (e.g., compassion for these young fathers), we might become susceptible to an other division of roles. The young fathers, mothers and children are the victims. The villains are cold-hearted politicians who immediately start chasing the fathers instead of trying to reunite the families – and the hero is the dialogue politician.

This brings us to the question: How do you respond to a frame that portrays you as a villain? The daddy tax/dialogue example makes clear what the answer to this question is: Present a different narrative, about the same situation or the same problem, in which the villain becomes the hero.

Kevin Rudd and Australia's boat people

In 2013, Australian prime minister Kevin Rudd announces that all asylum seekers who arrive in Australia by boat will henceforth be sent to neighboring Papua New Guinea, under a new agreement between the two countries. His left-wing opponents frame this as a disgraceful move and argue that he should be ashamed of "dumping" asylum seekers in one of the world's poorest and most poorly governed countries. The fact that Australia, as a rich and prosperous country, is effectively slamming the door in the face of some of the world's poorest and most marginalized people causes widespread outrage.

The division of roles in this frame is clear. The asylum seekers are the victims, Rudd is the villain, and the politicians attacking him and protecting asylum seekers are the heroes. How does the prime minister reframe the debate? He presents an alternative narrative that focuses on a different aspect of the same issue. According to Rudd, the country's dire refugee problem is caused by unscrupulous people smugglers who are charging asylum seekers a fortune to dump them on Australia's coast after an extremely dangerous journey across the Indian Ocean.

> Australians have had enough
> of seeing asylum seekers dying in the waters
> to our north and our northwest.
> They've had enough of people smugglers
> profiting from death. [...].
> I also have a message
> for the people smugglers in our region of the world:
> Your business model is over.[12]

Figure 4. Reframing the victim-villain-hero model

In Rudd's reframe, the asylum seekers are still victims, but the villains are now the people smugglers, who have made a business out of the refugees' suffering. And Prime Minister Rudd? He becomes the hero who is challenging these villains, destroying their business model, and tackling the root cause of the problem. In addition to this, the original hero – the parties opposing Rudd's policy – might become supporters of the villain: with their criticism on Rudd, they support the people smugglers.

The European Union and the pensioners of Cyprus

In 2013, Cyprus's banks face imminent collapse. The European Union (EU) comes to the country's aid, providing a much-needed bailout package, but insists that ordinary Cypriots would have to contribute to the recapitalization of the island's banking sector. As a result, it is agreed that deposits up to 100,000 euros will be guaranteed but that larger deposits will be subject to a substantial one-off levy. This is particularly painful for the Cypriots. Many of those with deposits worth over 100,000 euros were often just people saving for their pensions.

The terms of the bailout are drafted by the European ministers of finance under the leadership of their chairman, Jeroen Dijsselbloem, who subsequently faces questions from journalists regarding the terms of the agreement. What does he think of the fact that people who have been building up their pensions for many years now stand to lose a large chunk of their savings, plunging them into uncertainty in their twilight years?

It is a question that casts the EU in the role of the villain. The victims are the country's ordinary, diligent savers. The heroes are those who question the terms of the bailout.

How does Dijsselbloem respond to this frame?[13] By not stepping into it, but by presenting a different narrative based on the same facts. According to his version, the problem was that Cyprus's banking sector is too large and attracts too much illegal capital, in particular from Russia. Without the EU's intervention the banks would have collapsed and the country would have fallen into the abyss. The EU has done everything in its power to help Cyprus and the Cypriots. It will be clear, in this reframe, the villains are those who perpetuated this bloated and corrupt system – the banks, the Cypriot authorities, and money launderers from Russia and other countries. The hero is the EU, which secured the best possible deal for Cyprus under almost impossible circumstances.

What is the impact of this role reversal?

A villain-victim-hero frame always paints a very clear picture: there is a victim, you are a villain, and I am a hero. However, when someone counters the frame by presenting a different narrative based on the same facts, that picture becomes more ambiguous. The best-case scenario for designated villains is that this different narrative will dominate the debate and that they emerge as the new heroes. If that doesn't work, they still have a good chance of blurring the original division of roles because there are apparently other ways of looking at the facts.

More importantly, this strategy provides further proof that framing can contribute to the quality of political debates. Politics is all about perspective, and reframing through role reversal demonstrates that it is possible and legitimate to interpret the same facts in a variety of ways. Reframing is therefore more than a rhetorical trick: it provides the public with several different perspectives on an issue and might be helpful in deciding which one it likes best. If you don't agree with a villain-victim-hero narrative because it does not do justice to the complexity of the real world, try to reframe it by designing your own narrative. That might be much more effective than stating that your opponent's narrative is too simple.

5. Playing with your opponent's values

Margaret Thatcher and the gap between the rich and the poor

In 1990, Margaret Thatcher steps down as prime minister of the United Kingdom, after serving in the role for over a decade. In her final parliamentary debate as prime minister, the discussion focuses on the record of her Conservative government. During the debate a member of the Opposition, Simon Hughes, claims that Thatcher's policies have led to a huge increase in the gap between rich and poor:

> During her eleven years as Prime Minister,
> the gap between the richest 10 per cent
> and the poorest 10 per cent in this country
> has widened substantially.
> At the end of her chapter of British politics,
> how can she say
> that she can justify the fact that many people in a constituency such as mine
> are relatively much poorer,
> much less well housed
> and much less well provided for
> than they were in 1979?
> Surely she accepts
> that that is not a record
> that she or any prime minister
> can be proud of.

This is a classic left-wing frame. It claims that the conservative laissez-faire policy does nothing to control market forces, allowing the rich to become richer at the expense of the poor. Hughes holds Thatcher personally responsible for this state of affairs. So how does she reframe the debate? Thatcher says:

> People on all levels of income
> are better off than they were in 1979!
> The honorable Gentleman is saying
> that he would rather that the poor were poorer,
> provided that the rich were less rich.
> That way one will never create
> the wealth for better social services,
> as we have.
> What a policy!
> Yes, he would rather have the poor poorer,
> provided that the rich were less rich.

As the House of Commons erupts in uproar, there is no stopping her. In response to a subsequent question, Thatcher returns to her previous theme: "I must have hit the right nail on the head when I pointed out that the logic of those policies is that they would rather the poor were poorer."[1]

The frame used by Thatcher's opponents is that the rich have become richer while the poor have become poorer. Thatcher reframes the debate by pointing out that both sides have actually become richer. As a matter of fact, she argues, anyone who wants to narrow the wealth gap is basically in favor of making everyone poorer.

Using the downsides of your opponent's values

One of the aims of this book is to identify strategies and patterns in the game of framing and reframing. So what is the underlying pattern in this particular case?

Once again, it's all about the parties' values. Thatcher's non-conservative opponents place a strong emphasis on the principles of equality and equal opportunity. In their opinions, Thatcher's policies, which have widened the gap between the rich and the poor, are incompatible with those values.

In contrast, Thatcher's value pattern revolves around the free market, which, together with small government, facilitates enterprise and wealth creation.

There's something special about values. Almost no one is opposed to values like equality and equal opportunities. If a young person from a wealthy background and a young person from a poor background are equally talented, it's only fair that that they should have an equal chance of going to university. Likewise, almost everyone supports the idea of the free market. Society cannot function without entrepreneurs or competition – and successful entrepreneurs should be able to profit from their success.

However, every value also has a downside – values stand for something positive, but also for something negative, as demonstrated in Table 2.

Table 2. Values and downsides of values of four political ideologies

Political ideology	Core value	Downside
Socialism	Equal opportunities	Mediocrity
Conservatism	Free market	Sink-or-swim society
Liberalism	Individualism	Indifference
Christian-democracy	Communitarianism	Paternalism

The downside of the principle of equal opportunity is that it can lead to a second-rate society in which lower standards are the norm and excellence goes unrewarded. Anyone who supports this principle therefore risks encouraging a culture of mediocrity.

Similarly, the downside of principle of the free market is that it can give rise to a sink-or-swim society in which 10-15 percent of the population live below the poverty line. Anyone who is in favor of the free market must be prepared to accept this. In many cases, it is the downside of a politician's values rather than the values themselves that arouse opposition. When it is clear that the opponents' opinions and stances rely heavily on their underlying values, you can reframe the debate in two steps:

1. Point out the downsides of your opponent's values. This is what Thatcher does: Equality leads to mediocrity and a lack of social mobility.
2. Provide concrete examples of the impact of those downsides on your opponents values. In this particular case, Thatcher argues that mediocrity results in lower wages across the board. When this happens, she adds, the government also collects less tax revenue, which will result in less money for social services.

Figure 5. Playing with the downsides of the opponent's values

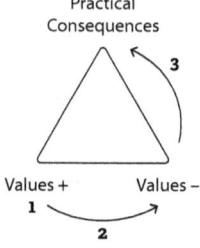

Incidentally, her opponent uses the exact same strategy – people in his constituency are "much poorer, much less well housed and much less well provided for" than they were before Thatcher came to power. This is, of course, the result of Thatcher's values: her strong emphasis on the free market will result in a sink-or-swim society

Figure 5 illustrates the essence of this strategy: (1) point out the downsides of your opponent's values; and (2) provide concrete examples of the impact of those downsides. If you only point out the downsides of your opponents values (Step 1), your argument will be too abstract. You must also convince your audience that these downsides lead to bad practical consequences that have a negative impact on daily life. In contrast, if you only talk about practical issues and daily life (Step 2), your criticism of your opponent will sound too arbitrary. "No," Thatcher might say, "it's no coincidence that my opponents' policies would make everyone poorer and result in less money for social services. This is clearly due to the values on which their policies are based." "No," her opponents might respond, "it's no accident that Thatcher's policies have led to a rise in poverty. This is a logical consequence of her values." By suggesting that something is not a coincidence, this strategy has the added thrill of unmasking one's opponents. Thatcher's conclusion of the debate on the wealth gap, after the statement that her opponents will make both the rich and the poor poorer, was:

> Yes, it came out!
> The honourable Member did not intend it to,
> but it did.[2]

Other examples

There are numerous other examples of this strategy. Ask civil servants at a transportation authority what their core values are. They will probably say something about reliability and predictability, which are, of course, very important values when you work on the nation's infrastructure. What might be a disadvantage of these values? Probably a lack of creativity. So when you frame a transportation authority as insufficiently creative and you can give concrete examples of this, many people will intuitively recognize this as inherent to the authority's values – and will therefore be more susceptible to this message.

Or take researchers working at a university. What values do people generally associate with university researchers? Probably "independence" and "objectivity." A university researcher is intellectually autonomous and is interested in the facts, not in opinions. These values also have their downsides: independent researchers can be framed as inhabitants of an ivory tower, completely disconnected from the real world, dealing with theoretical concepts and abstract ideas. Anyone who enters into a debate with a researcher can easily activate these downsides – the stance of the researcher is too theoretical, has nothing to do with the real world. Many observers will instinctively recognize this as inherent to the researcher's core values. If you are also able to provide them with concrete examples of the impact of these downsides, this framing strategy might be very effective.

Hijacking your opponent's values

There is a second way to play with your opponent's values: you can hijack these values. Hijacking means that you refer to the values or that you even take possession of them – your policies serve the values of your opponent.

Marco Rubio and immigration

In 2013, the US Senate is considering a proposal to grant citizenship to 11 million illegal immigrants. The Republicans are strongly opposed to this proposal, which they define as a typical left-liberal policy, condoning illegal behavior. To the consternation of many of them, Marco Rubio, a first-term Republican senator from Florida, votes in favor of the proposal. Many right-wing voters are furious – their conservative Senator takes a left-liberal stance on immigration. How does Rubio frame his support for this proposal?

> I know firsthand
> that while immigrants have always impacted America,
> America changes immigrants even more.
> Just a generation ago,
> my parents lived in poverty in another country.
> But America changed them.

> It gave them a chance to improve their lives.
> It gave them the opportunity to open doors
> for me and my siblings
> that had been closed for them.
> And the longer they lived here,
> the older their kids got,
> the more conservative they became.
> The more convinced they became
> that limited government,
> free enterprise
> and our constitutional liberties
> made this nation special.
> I am a witness
> to the transformative power of our country.
> How it doesn't change people's pocketbooks,
> it changes their hearts and minds.[3]

The essence of this reframe is that Rubio connects his left-liberal stance on this policy issue to conservative values – limited government, free enterprise and constitutional liberties – and the emotions underlying these values, such as a strong belief in the American dream and the transformative power of America. Why is this frame so powerful? First, as explained in Chapter 3, values help you establish a relationship with people. They help you reach their hearts and minds – in this case, the hearts and minds of conservative Republicans. By appealing to traditional right-wing values, Rubio can make his message more palatable to them.

Second, he makes things difficult for his opponents – in this case fellow Republicans who voted against the legalization of illegal immigrants – by referencing the same values as they do. In essence, he hijacks their core values. This is the second way of playing with values: connect your policy stance to your opponents values – and you can perhaps reach their hearts and minds, making it more difficult for them to successfully fight you.

Figure 6. Hijacking the opponent's values

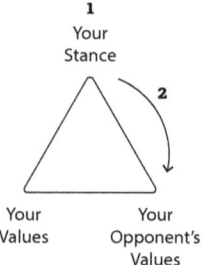

Ronald Reagan's Bear in the Woods

In 1984, Ronald Reagan is seeking reelection as president of the United States. In the foreign policy arena, he is known as the president who embodies hawkish values: there is a clear distinction between good (the USA) and evil (the Soviet Union) and that strong leadership requires decisiveness and a willingness to subdue the Russians from a position of power and military strength.

The opposite of this is a dovish value system, which argues that the distinction between good and evil is not always so clear-cut in real life – in other words, that good people can do bad things and bad people can do good things. According to this approach, leadership is chiefly about bridging differences, establishing relationships, and seeking interaction. A good leader needs to be flexible and willing to discuss or question his or her own positions.

A hawkish leader always comes up with powerful statements. A dovish leader dares to ask questions. How can hawks use the strategy of hijacking the values of their opponents? Of connecting a hawkish stance to dovish values?

Reagan explains his position on Russia in a short and famous campaign ad, "Bear in the Woods," in which he taps into dovish values. The ad, about the danger posed by Russia, paints a surprisingly peaceful picture. A bear roams through the woods, close to a man who happens to be walking there. The narrator says:

There is a bear in the woods.
For some people, the bear is easy to see.
Others don't see it at all.
Some people say the bear is tame.
Others say it's vicious and dangerous.
Since no one can really be sure who's right,
isn't it smart to be as strong as the bear?
If there is a bear.[4]

The bear in this scenario is obviously the Russian bear. So is this a hawkish narrative? Absolutely not. Reagan successfully cloaks his hawkish views in dovish values. Instead of a clear-cut distinction between good and evil, there is doubt all over. There may or may not be a bear. It may or may not be dangerous. The narration is gentle. The bear is not aggressive and simply roams about. Instead of a powerful message, the ad ends with a question: "Isn't it smart to be as strong as the bear?"

Why is this frame so powerful? Once again, values help you capture people's hearts and minds. In this case, they suggest that Reagan may be much less of a hawk than people might think. But there is more to this frame. By appealing to dovish values, Reagan also manages to hijack his opponents' values. According to his campaign ad, you can hold dovish values and reject a dualistic view of the United States's relations with Russia and still support Reagan's policies. By linking your policies to your opponent's values, you can break their monopoly on those values.

Other examples

Such hijacking of core values also occurs in other contexts. A typical left-wing value is to care about the unemployed and ensure that they receive adequate social services. In contrast, right-wing parties claim that they are the true champions of the unemployed, precisely because they want to lower unemployment benefits. They argue that lower benefits lead to better job opportunities and that, instead of turning the unemployed into lazy scroungers, they will get them back into work. So who is really looking after the unemployed in this scenario?

People on the left of the political spectrum are more likely to support tough environmental policies than their right-wing counterparts. So how can left-wing politicians drum up support for such policies on the right? The answer is simple: by linking environmental policies to right-wing values, such as strengthening the economy and promoting enterprise and innovation. According to this narrative, right-wing politicians who oppose environmental policies are effectively blocking economic growth and squandering opportunities for innovation.

How to reframe?

How to reframe when your opponent exploits the downsides of your values? Or when an opponent has hijacked your core values? The answer is fairly simple: keep reiterating your own values. When Marco Rubio hijacks your conservative values to defend a left-wing position, defend those values but argue that he is betraying them. Illegal immigrants have broken the law, but Rubio wants to reward them by granting them citizenship. When Ronald Reagan invokes dovish values to defend his hawkish position, defend those values but argue that he is and always has been a hawk. Tell your audience that presenting a left-wing position as a right-wing one, or a hawkish position as a dovish one, is a form of deception. Is a conservative politician suggesting that your left-wing values result in a mediocre society? Stick to your values – and make clear how these values have improves the lives of many people.

At the end of the previous chapters, I noted that the game of framing and reframing can raise the quality of political debate. In politics, every issue is always open to various perspectives and interpretations. A similar lesson emerges from this chapter. By using your opponent's values, you can cast an issue in an entirely different light. Conservative policies do not make the rich richer at the expense of the poor. Left-wing environmental policies also promote enterprise and innovation. A political dove can support increased defense spending. Again, framing is more than just a trick or opportunistic spinning – it can help to discover sometimes surprising new perspectives and can thus enrich the political debate.

6. Playing with opposite perspectives

Theresa May: I am leading a country

In 2017, the British Conservative prime minister Theresa May is the first foreign leader who visits president Donald Trump. In the first weeks of his presidency, Trump has signed an executive order, banning foreign nationals of a number of Muslim countries from visiting the US. UK citizens who have ties with these countries could also be denied entry to the US. By the way, his opponents frame his order as a "Muslim ban," the administration frames it as "extreme vetting" and the more neutral observers prefer to call it a "travel ban."

Furthermore, Trump has been very critical about NATO. May is working on Brexit, and might need a new trade deal with the US. She also invited Trump to a official state visit.

Labour leader Jeremy Corbyn wants the state visit to be canceled:

> President Trump
> has torn up international agreements on refugees,
> he has threatened to dump international agreements on climate change,
> he has praised the use of torture,
> he is inciting hatred against Muslims,
> he directly attacked women's rights.
> What more does president Trump has to do
> before the prime minister will listen
> to the near 1.8 million people
> who have already called
> for his state visit invitation to be withdrawn?

How does Theresa may respond? The core of Corbyn's foreign policy is, according to May,

> to object to
> and insult
> the democratically-elected head of state
> of our most important ally.
> Let's just see what he would have achieved in the last week.
> Would he have been able to protect British citizens
> from the impact of the executive order?
> No!
> Would he have been able
> to lay the foundations of a trade deal?
> No!
> Would he have got a 100 per cent commitment to NATO?
> No!
> That's what Labour has to offer this country,
> less protection for British citizens,
> less prosperous,
> less safe.
> He can lead a protest,
> I'm leading a country.[1]

The game of opposites

What is happening here? Jeremy Corbyn has a normative or idealistic stance: It is morally wrong to invite Trump for a state visit. May does not enter into this frame – she reframes the debate into a discussion about the real world, about the facts. She does not want to talk about morals, but about reality. The language of idealism, which focuses on justness, is replaced with the language of realism – which focuses on results. A moral frame is replaced with a factual frame. From this factual perspective, Corbyn is suddenly a very naïve politician, who "can lead a protest," but not a country.

Figure 7. Playing with opposite perspectives

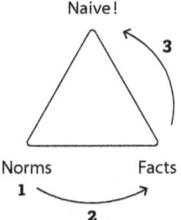

A normative perspective is the antithesis of a factual perspective, which is why I call this strategy of changing perspectives, "playing with opposite perspectives." The game always follows the same pattern. When you are confronted with a frame based on a particular perspective, you can reframe the debate by switching to its polar opposite. In addition to the above mentioned fact-value distinction, there are several other opposite pairs that crop up all the time in political debates.

Content versus process frames

Mark Rutte and the EU
In many EU member states, people are critical of the European Union, especially at the conservative end of the political spectrum. The Dutch conservative prime minister, Mark Rutte is very critical of Europe in the Netherlands, in order to keep his conservative supporters happy – at least, according to his opponents. His opponents also state that Rutte turns into a European loyalist who doesn't voice any criticism at all, as soon as he arrives in the EU capitol, Brussels. The picture is clear: the prime minister is a political opportunist who blows with the prevailing wind. In the United States they would call him a flip-flopper.

A member of Rutte's party seeks to defend Rutte's record by explaining that Rutte's tougher position in the Netherlands actually serves the softer approach in Europe and Brussels.

If you always say 'yes' in Brussels,
people start to like you.
And when you occasionally say 'no,'
they are prepared to take you seriously.
People take Mark seriously in Europe.[2]

If you place Rutte's views on Europe in a content frame, you are left with an opportunist who says one thing when he is at home and another thing when he is in Brussels. However, Rutte's party members reframe the debate by placing the prime minister's seemingly contradictory statements in an opposite frame: this is not about the content of the prime minister's stances, this is about the process of negotiation in Brussels. A politician who is highly critical of Europe at home is obviously much more likely to succeed in the Brussels negotiations than one who constantly praises the European Union. If you place Rutte's two-faced attitude toward the European Union in a content frame, he comes off as an opportunist and a flip-flopper. However, if you place the same attitude in a process frame, he appears to be a tough and smart negotiator who strengthens his position by criticizing Europe, thus achieving the best possible deal for the Netherlands. In this way, he has more influence than many pro-European parties, whose negotiating positions are probably much weaker. Also, in this process frame, the prime minister's opponents are suddenly very naïve – they don't understand that you'll have to negotiate in Brussels and that the prime minister is a very good negotiator.

Figure 8. Playing with opposite perspectives: Content versus process

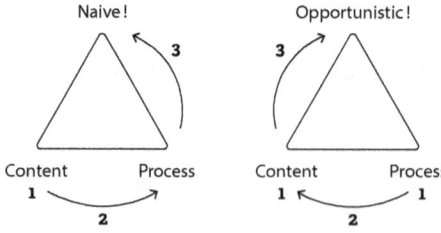

What is the reframe of the reframe here? Refer to the original frame. The prime minister is presented as a good negotiator (process), but does not have a clear vision (content). Without a clear vision you cannot negotiate or without a clear vision everything is negotiable, and you will develop into an opportunist.

Policy versus political frames

Barack Obama, policy and politics
In November 2010, the United States holds an important mid-term election in which the Democrats suffer heavy losses. One of the main reasons for this outcome is dissatisfaction with the Obama administration. The economy is in bad shape, and many of Obama's election promises have been watered down. In an interview with the *New York Times*, the president reflected on this dissatisfaction:

> We probably spend much more time
> trying to get the policy right
> than trying to get the politics right.[3]

The president thus appears to operate in two different arenas: the policy arena and the political arena. Table 3 sums up the key differences between these two worlds.

Table 3. Differences between the political arena and the policy arena

Politics	Policy
Setting the agenda	Implementing the agenda
Sense and simplicity	High tolerance of complexity
Differences	Commonalities
Principles	Pragmatism

In the political arena, what matters most is setting the agenda. What are the key problems facing society and how should they be solved? The aim is to convince the electorate that the problems politicians have identified are the biggest problems that should be driving the agenda. In the policy arena, the focus is on how to implement the solutions to these problems and translate them into effective action. The issues here are very different and include such obstacles as obstructive stakeholders, legal barriers, and new information that changes the way a problem is viewed. In short, politically motivated politicians set the agenda, while policy-oriented politicians focus on implementation.

A high tolerance for complexity is essential in the policy arena, because policy-oriented politicians can only be truly effective if they are willing to confront the intricacies of the real world. In the political arena, however, the opposite often applies. Politically motivated politicians regularly try to distill complicated matters to their essence, as complex messages are difficult to communicate.

In the political arena, it is important to differentiate yourself from others. Because voters need to have a choice, differences between parties need to be accentuated. In the policy arena, however, practicalities matter more than principles, and clarity is less important than a willingness to make concessions. Real-life problems cannot be solved without a certain amount of pragmatism and compromise.

This tension between politics and policy can be used in the game of framing and reframing. When a policy-oriented politician is placed in a political frame, his or her sensible pragmatism is quickly recast as evidence of a lack of principle. By the same token, when a politically motivated politician is placed in a policy frame, he or she is recast as an ideological "all talk, no action" politician, who never gets anything done.

Geert Wilders: We are succumbing to Islam
An example. Like many Western countries, the Netherlands offers citizenship courses that are designed to acquaint immigrants with the history, values, and customs of their new home. In the historic Dutch town of Utrecht, however, a group of Muslim women refuses to attend their local citizenship course because they do not wish to study in mixed-gender class on religious and cultural grounds. A local politician who attaches great

importance to these nonmandatory courses comes up with a practical solution: women-only classes. Such classes will draw the women out of their isolation and introduce them to Dutch society. It is the kind of pragmatic solution one might expect from a practical, policy-oriented politician.

Geert Wilders, the leader of the Netherlands's anti-immigrant and anti-Muslim Freedom Party, responds to this proposal as follows.

> The town of Utrecht
> is offering gender-segregated classes,
> one classroom for men and another one for women.
> What is the key message here?
> We are willing to succumb
> to their desert ideology.

Wilders places the practical policy solution of offering women-only classes in a political frame: separated classes amount to an acceptance of the idea that men and women are not equal. The underlying strategy will be clear. There is a pragmatic solution that works. Put this solution in a policy frame – and it will be valued positively. Put it in a political frame, and pragmatism is turned into a betrayal of principles.

It is also possible to use the strategy in an opposite way: a stance that is valued positively in a political frame might have a negative connotation in a policy frame. A policy-oriented politician could argue that the Freedom Party is very political and that it never manages to solve any problems.

Figure 9. Playing with opposing perspectives: Policy versus politics

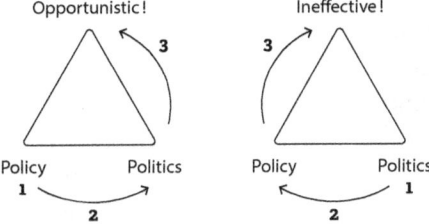

Anyone who understands this dynamic can see that politicians need to have a foot in both frames. A policy-oriented politician must also have a political frame available, and a politically motivated politician needs policy frames – needs to offer practical solutions. If you don't have frames rooted in both worlds, you can easily lose a debate.

Idealistic versus realistic frames

This strategy was already introduced with help of the example of May and Corbyn. It is a frequently used strategy, in particular along the divide between conservative and liberal parties.

Some left-wing parties like to advocate tax increases for high earners. These proposals are usually based on an underlying political ideal: the broadest shoulders should carry the greatest burden. Politicians who oppose such proposals risk exposing themselves to a flood of moral criticism that accuses them of making the rich richer at the expense of the poor and creating a ruthless sink-or-swim society in which only the fittest are able to survive. If you want to avoid such criticism, the most effective strategy is to reframe the debate by placing ideals in a realist frame. For example, you can highlight the fact that higher taxes simply don't work in practice. On the contrary, they encourage tax avoidance and make countries less attractive to foreign companies and investors. The implication is that this ideal looks great on paper but is unworkable in real life – it is naïve.

Mohamed ElBaradei: "You can't eat Sharia"

Egyptian politician Mohamed ElBaradei, a former head of the International Atomic Energy Agency (IAEA), is widely respected around the world as a supporter of liberalism and democracy.

The Egyptian army has just ousted the country's president, Mohamed Morsi, who is also the leader of the fundamentalist Muslim Brotherhood. Morsi became president after free and democratic elections. Ousting a democratically elected president is morally wrong, so the African Union immediately suspends Egypt from all its activities. ElBaradei, however, supports Morsi's removal. Howe can reconcile this position with his liberal and democratic principles?

The question is a normative one: Is it morally acceptable for an army to overthrow a democratically elected government? If ElBaradei steps into this normative frame, he will almost certainly lose. He will either have to admit that he acted undemocratically in supporting Morsi's ouster or he will have to deny that the ouster itself was undemocratic. Both options will make him look bad, so how does he reframe the debate?

> Egypt is already a failed state.
> The evidence is all around us.
> Today you see an erosion of state authority in Egypt.
> The state is supposed to provide security and justice,
> that's the most basic form of statehood.
> But law and order is disintegrating.
> The feeling right now
> is that there is no state authority
> to enforce law and order.

And how did things get to this? According to ElBaradei, the reason is that Morsi's government has "no clue how to run Egypt."

> It's not a question of whether they are Muslim Brothers or liberals,
> it's a question of people who have no vision or experience.
> They do not know how to diagnose the problem
> and then provide the solution.
> They are simply not qualified to govern.

ElBaradei sums his concerns up nicely with a catchy one-liner:

> You can't eat Sharia.[4]

ElBaradei reframes the debate about Morsi's removal from a normative debate (is it morally right to remove a democratically elected government?) to a debate about the facts (has this government the competencies to manage the country?). It no longer matters whether or not the army's intervention was morally justified. The fact is that Egypt has become a failed state. When the government is incapable of running the country and state institutions stop functioning, questions about democratic legitimacy become irrelevant.

Realism is immoral, is fatalism

You can also reverse this strategy: if your opponents rely on a realist frame, you can make them look cold-hearted and cynical by placing their argument in an idealistic frame. Opponents of military intervention often claim that such action has few long-term benefits. Even if you manage to remove a dictator from power, it may subsequently be impossible to establish democratic institutions or keep a lid on sectarian violence. This argument – military intervention doesn't work – is based on a realist approach. You can reframe the debate by placing the issue in an idealistic frame, for example, by asking your opponents why they are opposed to protecting people from a brutal dictator. Protecting people is a moral obligation. How can they be so cold-hearted?

Figure 10.   Playing with opposing perspectives: Normative versus factual

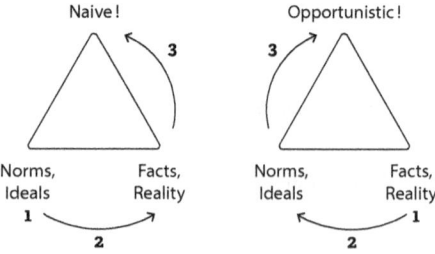

Very close to this strategy of reframing realism is another reframe: redefine realism as fatalism. We sometimes see this in the debate about immigration. A politician might state that we have to be realistic – immigrants will keep coming, given climate change, given a lack of opportunities for young people in poor countries. We should not look the other way. Realistic? Might the reframe be "This is a fatalistic stance"? "Fatalism is immoral" might be the next step in the storyline, "fatalism is a cynical stance." It means that we accepts things as the are, irrespective of the consequences.

Strategic versus operational frames

The final pair of opposites consists of strategy versus operations. The following passage on long-term developments in the health-care industry is typical of strategic white papers on such issues.

> The health-care industry is facing several unavoidable developments. Over the coming decades, demand for services will increase dramatically. This is partly due to population aging and partly to technological innovation, which contributes to the availability of new forms of treatment. All this will also lead to substantial cost increases.
> In this new reality, everyone wants the highest available level of care at an affordable price. Any health-care organization that is unable to provide full transparency with regard to the quality and cost of its services has little chance of survival. All organizations will have to introduce systems specifying their level of performance and how it is measured.

This is proper strategic language: long-term developments, fundamental change, dramatic change with inevitable consequences, requiring the introduction of performance-measurement systems in the health-care industry.

Opponents of such systems who steps into this strategic frame are taking a risk. Their objections can simply be dismissed as the rearguard actions of those who lack vision and fail to identify major strategic trends. It is therefore much more effective to present this position using an operational frame. The resulting message looks very different:

> What will happen when doctors are forced to record and measure all their actions? Performance measurement systems will lead to more bureaucracy and hassle. Moreover, these systems always have perverse effects, such as encouraging calculating behavior by doctors. This is simply the latest example of excessive managerial intrusion, which undermines professional autonomy and ultimately leads to the deprofessionalization of the health-care industry.

When placed in an operational frame, the arguments of the strategic thinker suddenly sound naïve and superficial. They are divorced from reality and seem to consist of meaningless management-speak and strategic buzzwords. It also works the other way around. When you place an operational argument in a strategic frame, it can suddenly sound trivial and petty.

Figure 11. Playing with opposite perspectives: Strategy versus operations

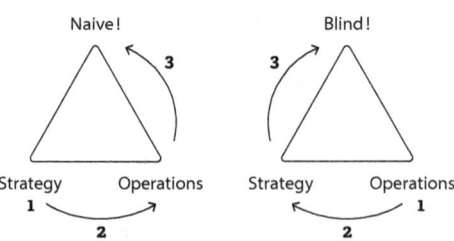

Again, this is clearly more than just a game. Anyone who presents a strategic vision should also be required to address its operational consequences, and anyone who focuses on operational processes should also have the courage to address long-term, strategic developments.

How to reframe an opposing perspective?

There are undoubtedly many more pairs of competing approaches that can be used in the game of framing and reframing. In essence, the game of opposites consists of two steps:

1. Figure out what type of frame your opponents are using to convey their message. Is it, for example, a substantive frame, a vision, is it about ideals or strategy?
2. Place your opponents' message in a frame that is the polar opposite of the one they are using. This gives their message an entirely different meaning. In a content frame, the Dutch prime minister comes off as a opportunistic flip-flopper on issues relating to the European Union, but in a process frame he is a tough negotiator. A message that appears to convey depth and understanding when placed in a strategic frame suddenly sounds naïve and superficial when placed in an operational frame.

How to reframe?

First of all, if your opponent reframes you with an opposing perspective, simply stick to your original frame. If you are in favor of higher taxes (idealism) and your opponent's response is that your proposal is unrealistic – stick to your frame, emphasizing that your opponent is not realistic, but cynical or underambitious.

Second and more importantly, have a foot in both frames. Politicians who are in favor of higher taxes on moral grounds (idealism) can make things harder for their opponents by also placing their message in a realist frame.

Bill Clinton on equality

Bill Clinton does exactly that when he calls for greater economic equality:

> It turns out that advancing equal opportunity
> and economic empowerment
> is both morally right
> and good economics.
> Why?
> Because poverty, discrimination and ignorance restrict growth.
> When you stifle human potential,
> when you don't invest in new ideas,
> it doesn't just cut off the people who are affected,
> it hurts us all.[5]

Having a foot in both frames, makes you less vulnerable for this strategy – and your opponents more vulnerable, of they emphasize just one of the opposing perspectives.

Framing with dilemmas

In a slightly different version of playing with opposites, opposing frames can also be treated as a dilemma. Should you focus on content or process? Probably, most people will come up with an "on the one hand, on the other hand" answer. On the one hand, you need to present a clear position on key issues (content). On the other hand, you need room to maneuver in order to negotiate effectively (process). The best option is therefore to focus on content and process. Should you focus on strategy or operations? On the one hand, you need to have a strategic vision. On the other hand, you need to take account of how things work in practice. The best option is therefore to focus on strategy and operations.

What role can dilemmas play in the game of framing and reframing?

Ecstasy and pill checks

MDMA or ecstasy is a party drug that is popular at all-night dance parties. The chemical composition of MDMA pills, which are illegal to buy and sell, can differ enormously. Some of these pills are extremely dangerous. From time to time, people actually die from taking them.

In northern Europe, whenever this happens, it fuels a debate about government responsibility. Should local authorities provide partygoers with a means to test the safety of MDMA pills before taking them? This raises an interesting dilemma. On the one hand, everyone wants to prevent fatalities, and testing can prevent people from taking dangerous pills. On the other hand, any government that allows such testing at the very least implies that it condones MDMA use.

Now, suppose that you are opposed to such tests but you obviously don't want people to die, either. In that case, this might be an effective frame:

> Tests create a false sense of security.
> Whether or not you die from using MDMA
> does not just depend on the chemical composition
> of a particular pill
> but also on your level of physical fitness.
> If you are not in top physical condition,
> any MDMA pill can kill you.

Why is this "false sense of security" frame so powerful? First of all, it offers us a way out of the above-mentioned dilemma. Anyone who cares strongly about both sides of the issue will welcome a frame that offers them a way out. They will only be too happy to believe that testing creates a false sense of security.

Second, it is impossible to accuse the user of this frame of not caring about potential victims, on the one hand, or of condoning

MDMA use, on the other. This is because the issue is no longer about the pros and cons of testing. The user of the frame has managed to transcend the entire dilemma by arguing that the tests themselves only provide a false sense of security. Figure 12 has the essence of this strategy.

Figure 12. Framing with dilemmas

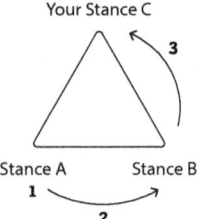

Immigration

This framing strategy is also frequently used in the debate on immigration. Imagine that a famine or an armed conflict is creating a huge stream of refugees. One country has already absorbed a large number of refugees, and the question now is whether it should accept any more. Consider the following frame:

> On the one hand, we have a moral duty to help these people.
> On the other hand, our country has already done its fair share.
> If we absorb any more refugees,
> society will collapse under the pressure.
> We should care for these people in the region,
> thus keeping them close to home.

What does this "close to home" frame achieve? First of all, it presents the refugee problem as a moral dilemma. Second, once we acknowledge the existence of the dilemma, we become susceptible to the "close to home" frame, since it offers us a way out. In addition, we cannot accuse the owners of the frame of being cold and heartless, because they acknowledge that we have a moral duty to help refugees. However, this moral duty also creates a moral dilemma.

If you step into this frame to oppose the position it advocates – for example, on drug testing or caring for refugees in their own region – you expose yourself to various risks. You may be accused of seeing only half the problem and ignoring the dilemma. In contrast, the owner of the frame appears to transcend the dilemma – and is thus beyond criticism. Should we try to prevent drug-related fatalities? "Of course," says the owner of the frame, "but testing the chemical composition of MDMA pills is not the solution." Should we help refugees? "Absolutely," says the owner of the frame, "but we have already done our fair share and you can also help them closer to home."

How to reframe?

In order to successfully reframe a dilemma, simply you ensure that not your opponent, but you are the one who appears to rise above it. You can achieve this by redefining the dilemma:

- If you support MDMA pill tests, redefine the dilemma: on the one hand, they may not be 100 percent effective, on the other hand we have to do what we can to save lives.
- If you are in favor of a more liberal admission policy toward refugees, redefine the dilemma. On the one hand, refugees should be helped in the region where they come from, and on the other hand, the capacity of regional refugee centers might be limited, so accepting more refugees is the best way out.

By making your opponent's frame part of a new dilemma, you take away its power. The debate is now about the dilemma you have introduced, which you alone are able to transcend.

Figure 13.   Reframing with dilemmas

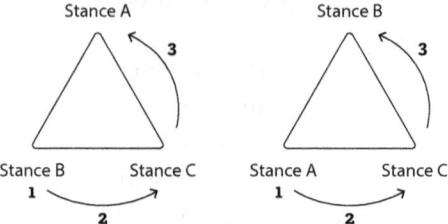

Political oxymorons

An oxymoron is a figure of speech that unites two contradictory concepts. "Organized chaos" is an oxymoron, because organization and chaos are each other's opposite. Oxymorons are a common feature of political discourse. Former Texas governor George achieved considerable success and popularity with his own brand of "compassionate conservatism," a phrase implying that the person in question is right-wing and conservative but not uncaring. He or she thus transcends the traditional distinction between the compassion of the left and the conservatism of the right.

Former UK prime minister David Cameron claimed to respect all the classic liberal freedoms, including for immigrants, but was willing to take firm action if any of those freedoms were abused. He described this approach as "muscular liberalism."[6]

Russia's deputy prime minister, Dmitry Rogozin, called himself a "peace hawk." A peace hawk is someone with a lot of military power, who is, however, not interested in waging war but in protecting the peace. It is a slightly different version of Ronald Reagan's motto "peace through strength."

Based on these examples, it is fairly easy to come up with a methodology for inventing a successful political oxymoron:

- Identify your own values: conservative, liberal, peaceful, or otherwise.

- Determine what negative response those values might evoke in society. For example, conservatism is often associated with an uncaring attitude, liberalism with weakness, and peacefulness with appeasement.
- Attach an adjective to your values that counteracts this negative response – compassionate conservatism, muscular liberalism, or peace hawk.

This is a classic thesis-antithesis-synthesis model that allows the politician in question to transcend the inherent contradiction of the oxymoron. Table 4 lists several more examples of political oxymorons.

Table 4. Examples of political oxymorons

Conservative environmentalist – Winfried Kreschmann, prime minister of Baden-Württemberg
Conservative feminist – Sarah Palin, US governor
Social liberal – Manuel Valls, prime minister of France
Big government conservative – Rick Santorum, US senator
Realistic socialist – Alexis Tsipras, prime minister of Greece
Green capitalist – François Fillon, prime minister of France
Global nationalist – Shinzō Abe, prime minister of Japan
Modern traditionalist – Narendra Modi, prime minister of India

There are several reasons why political oxymorons are such a useful and powerful language.

First, they resolve contradictions highlighted by others. The conservative Christian Social Union (CSU) in the German state of Bavaria refers to itself as the party of "laptops and lederhosen" because it champions traditional values (lederhosen, traditional leather trousers) as well as innovation (laptops). But aren't these two things polar opposites? "No," says the CSU, "our traditional values actually serve as a basis for innovation."

Second, they hijack your opponents' core values. US Democrats claim that compassion for the weakest members of society is one of their party's core values, while Republicans firmly believe in the wisdom of the market. "That is not accurate," counters George W. Bush, "because I am a compassionate conservative."

Third, the owners of these oxymorons are hard to pin down. Oxymorons are by definition ambiguous and leave room for interpretation. For example, it is difficult to articulate what a term like "social liberal" means, and that is precisely what makes it so effective. People can interpret it however they like.

Fourth, oxymorons might be liberating. According to political oxymorons, social engagement and conservatism are not mutually exclusive. Likewise, liberalism is not always synonymous with leniency. In fact, there is also such a thing as "muscular liberalism."

Fifth, they might be innovative. People who still think in terms of conventional political contradictions are behind the times. Dismissing those on the left as tree-hugging pacifists and those on the right as capitalist warmongers is an example of outdated thinking, since we now have muscular liberals and compassionate conservatives. Oxymorons imply that your opponents are still stuck in an old-fashioned mindset while you and your supporters have already moved on.

How to reframe?

There are, of course, various ways to reframe an oxymoron:

- Use the being-neither-here-nor-there frame. The use of oxymorons implies that politicians are afraid of making tough choices or that they are in the middle of an identity crisis. Because conservatism is no longer popular, they desperately slap the word "compassionate" in front of it. Because socialism had been discredited, they start referring to themselves as "social liberals."
- Unmask the oxymoron. When the chips are down, a "compassionate conservative" is first and foremost a conservative. When social liberals come under pressure, they always retreat to their earlier socialist positions.

- Use the facts of the case to undermine the oxymoron. Any policy proposal is always going to be more compassionate than conservative – or vice versa, or more social than liberal – or vice versa. If you highlight the true essence of the policy, the oxymoron evaporates into thin air.

Finally, as a side note, it worth mentioning that the supporters of a particular oxymoron will often deny that it constitutes a contradiction in terms. For example, a true conservative will often insist that conservatism is inherently compassionate, because a smaller safety net ensures that people are less reliant on the state and more likely to find work. This is much more compassionate than making them dependent on government handouts. Likewise, many people regard libertarian paternalism as an oxymoron, but others claim that libertarianism has always had a paternalistic streak. Is a "realistic socialist" an oxymoron? Socialists have always been very realistic, will many socialists say.

One significant conclusion drawn in the foregoing chapters was that framing can indeed contribute to the quality of the political debate. Playing the game of framing and reframing creates a range of perspectives on the same issue and this can enrich the debate and lead to better decision-making. Of course, framing can sometimes be a shallow political ruse, but it can also be more than that. And this is certainly also the conclusion we come to in this chapter. Each of the opposing perspectives on a given issue is legitimate and therefore the framing/reframing game can enrich the political debate as well as political decision-making.

7. Meta-framing

Newt Gingrich and CNN: "Trash like that"

In the run-up to the 2012 US presidential election, four candidates are competing in the Republican primaries. One of them is Mitt Romney, who will eventually go on to win his party's nomination. Another is the former Speaker of the House, Newt Gingrich. Just before a key primary debate in the conservative South, which will be broadcasted live by CNN, something interesting happens.

Years earlier, Gingrich's first marriage ended in divorce over his affair with another woman. This clearly does not help him in the conservative South, but it happened a long time ago and the American public has more or less forgiven him for it.

A few days before the debate, however, Gingrich's ex-wife reveals on *ABC News* that after she found out about the affair Gingrich suggested they have an open marriage. The story immediately goes viral. The big question is whether it will also come up during the debate.

Well, it does. At the very start of the debate, the moderator – John King – asks Gingrich if he wants to respond to his ex-wife's revelations:

> As you know,
> your ex-wife gave an interview to *ABC News*
> and another interview with the *Washington Post*.
> And this story has now gone viral on the internet.
> In it, she says that you came to her in 1999,
> at a time when you were having an affair.
> She says you asked her, sir,
> to enter into an open marriage.
> Would you like to take some time to respond to that?

King's framing of the issue is very tricky for Gingrich. Denying the allegation – "No, I did not propose an open marriage" – could easily have the opposite effect. How should Gingrich reframe the debate? He responds as follows:

> No,
> but I will.
> I think the destructive, vicious, negative nature
> of much of the news media
> makes it harder to govern this country,
> harder to attract decent people to run for public office.
> And I am appalled
> that you would begin a presidential debate
> on a topic like that.

He continues:

> Every person in here knows personal pain.
> Every person in here has had someone close to them
> go through painful things.
> To take an ex-wife
> and make it two days before the primary
> a significant question for a presidential campaign
> is as close to despicable
> as anything I can imagine. [...]
> I am frankly astounded
> that CNN would take trash like that
> and use it to open a presidential debate.

King receives the full blast of Gingrich's anger. If you watch a recording of the debate, you can actually see the blood drain from King's face. He tries to rescue the situation by acknowledging Gingrich's irritation while explaining that it wasn't CNN that interviewed his ex-wife. Gingrich needs to understand that it was ABC and that the story has since gone viral. However, his efforts are to no avail. Gingrich continues to tear into him:

John, John, it was repeated by your network.
You chose to start the debate with it.
Don't try to blame somebody else.
You and your staff chose to start this debate with it.
Let me be quite clear. The story is false.[1]

Gingrich claims that his friends and daughters all know the story is false. His daughters even asked ABC not to broadcast the interview, but it did so anyway. He also claims to be tired of the elite media, which is doing everything it can to protect the Democratic incumbent – Barack Obama – by portraying Republican candidates in a negative light.

Meta-framing: From "into" to "about"

Gingrich reframes the debate with two strategies that have already been discussed: the victim-villain-hero frame and uses the 3P model – I will come back to that. But there is more here.

Gingrich is also using the strategy of meta-framing: instead of stepping into his opponent's frame, Gingrich says something about the frame itself. King's question and frame is morally wrong, destructive and appalling. It violates the core values of good journalism, discourages people from running for public office, and ultimately harms democracy itself.

Figure 14.   Meta-framing

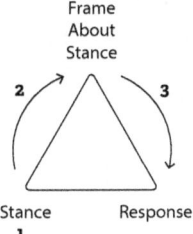

Gingrich's meta-framing has several effects. First of all, it completely changes the way we see the debate. The issue is no longer whether or not Gingrich suggested an open marriage but whether the media is behaving immorally and undermining democracy by discouraging a new generation of leaders from coming forward.

Second, once he has reframed the debate, Gingrich is free to return to the original question. He claims that his ex-wife's story isn't true – but simultaneously argues that it is no longer the key issue. What really matters is that CNN has used "trash like that" to open a presidential debate.

Third, once he has reframed the debate, Gingrich is free to use any of the other frames discussed in this book. In John King's frame, Gingrich's ex-wife is the victim and Gingrich is the villain. But the latter's meta-frame turns everything on its head. Now King is the villain, and Gingrich the hero, while decent people who just want to serve their country are the victims. The Republicans are also victims, because the elite media is constantly out to get them. Gingrich also makes use of the 3P model. He takes a deeply personal issue (marital infidelity) and turns it into a matter of principle (journalistic integrity).

Julia Gillard: "I will not be lectured by this man"

The next example takes us to the other side of the globe. In 2012, Julia Gillard is prime minister of Australia. The speaker of the Australian parliament, who supports Gillard's government, stands accused of sending several sexist text messages, which have become public. The conservative leader of the Opposition, Tony Abbott, tables a motion calling for the speaker's resignation – because sexism and misogyny are incompatible with such a position. Abbott thereby places Gillard in a very awkward position. On the one hand, she has spent her entire life waging war on sexism and therefore has no option but to condemn the speaker. On the other hand, she needs his support to maintain her party's parliamentary majority, which amounts to just one seat. Faced with an almost impossible choice, Gillard opts for a meta-framing strategy. This is her response to Abbott's proposal:

> I will not be lectured
> about sexism and misogyny
> by this man.
> I will not.
> And the Government will not be lectured
> about sexism and misogyny
> by this man.
> Not now, not ever.
> The Leader of the Opposition says
> that people who hold sexist views
> and who are misogynists
> are not appropriate for high office.
> Well I hope the Leader of the Opposition
> has got a piece of paper
> and he is writing out his resignation.
> Because if he wants to know
> what misogyny looks like in modern Australia,
> he doesn't need a motion in the House of Representatives,
> he needs a mirror.

Gillard provides several examples of Abbott's "double standards." For example, she notes that he said in an interview that he has no problem with the fact that women are underrepresented in senior positions because men are physiologically and temperamentally more suited to exercising authority. Then she gets personal:

> I was very offended personally
> when the Leader of the Opposition,
> as Minister of Health, said,
> and I quote, "Abortion is the easy way out."
> I was very personally offended
> by those comments. [...]

> I was also very offended
> on behalf of the women of Australia
> when the Leader of the Opposition said,
> "What the housewives of Australia need to understand as
> they do the ironing." [...]
> Thank you for that painting of women's roles in modern
> Australia. [...]
> I was offended when the Leader of the Opposition
> went outside in front of Parliament
> and stood next to a sign that said
> "Ditch the witch."
> I was offended when the Leader of the Opposition
> stood next to a sign
> that described me as a man's bitch.
> I was offended by those things.
> Misogyny, sexism,
> every day from this Leader of the Opposition.
> Every day in every way,
> across the time the Leader of the Opposition
> has sat in that chair and I've sat in this chair,
> that is all we have heard from him. [...]
> Well this kind of hypocrisy must not be tolerated,
> which is why this motion from the Leader of the Opposition
> should not be taken seriously.

On the subject of the speaker's text messages, Gillard eventually states:

> I am offended by their content
> because I am always offended by sexism. [...]
> I am offended by those things
> in the same way
> that I have been offended
> by things that the Leader of the Opposition has said.[2]

She then goes on to note that a court case is still in progress and that parliament should therefore await the judge's decision on the matter.

All in all, Gillard's strategy is very similar to the one used by Gingrich. First, she reframes the debate by using a meta-frame. Instead of stepping into Abbott's frame, she says something about the frame itself – It is morally unacceptable that the sexist Abbott complains about sexism and misogyny. This completely changes the way we see the debate. It is no longer about the speaker's sexist text messages but about Abbott's own sexism and double standards.

Second, only after she has reframed the debate – and all attention is focused on Abbott's sexism – does Gillard say anything about the issue that started the whole debate. She duly notes that she is offended by the Speaker's text messages and that she will abide by the judge's decision. However, the text messages have long stopped being the issue – it's now all about Abbott's double standards.

Third, like Gingrich, Gillard is free to use other framing strategies once she has reframed the debate. In Abbott's frame, the speaker of the Australian parliament is the villain and Abbot himself is the hero. However, when Gillard is done with him, Abbott has become the sexist villain who is no position to moralize and the victims are the women of Australia. There are also traces of the 3P model here. Gillard takes a debate about principles and makes it highly personal by highlighting Abbott's own double standards and emphasizing her own indignation.

Nonmoral meta-framing

The strength of both Gingrich's and Gillard's meta-framing strategy is their moral judgment of the frames used by their opponents. They not only change the topic of the debate, they also make it a debate about values and morality. However, it is also possible to use this strategy without appealing to values. In such cases, the purpose is simply to change the topic of the debate. In the following paragraphs, I examine some other frequently used examples of meta-framing.

Carter: The attitude Republicans always take

Accusing your opponent of always pushing the same narrative is a well-known meta-frame. In 1976, sitting US president Gerald Ford and his challenger, Jimmy Carter, are participating in a presidential debate. Ford promises to introduce several new programs in the fields of health care, housing, and leisure time. However, this will cost money, and Ford is also in favor of lowering taxes. The question is therefore how these two positions can be reconciled. Carter says,

> Mr. Ford takes the same attitude
> that the Republicans always take.
> In the last 3 months before an election,
> they are always for the programs
> that they fight the other 3½ years.[3]

This is a meta-frame. Instead of addressing the details of Ford's proposals, Carter says something about his position, by accusing him of taking the same attitude the Republicans always take. By meta-framing the issue, he seemingly exposes Ford's true character – a politician who promises, but already knows that he will not deliver.

Bush and Trump: "I am not a debater"

Some politicians are not good debaters. When George H. W. Bush takes on Democratic candidate Michael Dukakis during the 1988 US presidential election, it is clear that Dukakis is the better debater. Dukakis is a good speaker, and there is a strong chance that Bush will lose to him in key debates. Bush is aware of this, and even says so in his speech accepting the Republican nomination:

> It's been said that I am not the most compelling speaker.
> And there are actually those who claim
> that I don't always communicate in the clearest, most concise way. [...]
> Now I [...] may not be the most eloquent. [...]
> And I may sometimes be a little awkward,
> but there is nothing self-conscious in my love of country.
> And I am a quiet man [...]
> but I hear the quiet people others don't.
> The ones who raise the family, pay the taxes, meet the mortgage.
> And I hear them, and I am moved, and their concerns are mine.[4]

In 2015, Donald Trump announces that he is running for president of the United States. Despite being a successful businessman, he is a political outsider who will come up against several experienced politicians during the Republican primaries. Before his first big debate, the question on everyone's mind is therefore whether he will even survive the experience. Trump responds as follows:

> I'm not a debater.
> These politicians,
> I always say, they're all talk no action.
> They debate all the time.
> They go out and debate every night. I don't debate. [...]
> I've created tremendous jobs.
> I've built a great company.
> I do a lot of things.
> And maybe my whole life is a debate in a way.
> But the fact is I'm not a debater and they are.[5]

Prior to the debates in which they will participate, Bush and Trump both introduce a meta-frame by saying something about the debates before they enter into debate. If you watch the debates through the lens of this meta-frame, you see things in a very different light. Dukakis is highly educated, cold, and analytical, while Bush is straightforward and warm. Dukakis will probably win the debate, but the question is how much this matters. What is more important – that the president is a good debater or that he is a calm and honest person who is able to see the people that others don't? Trump is a successful businessman, a man of action, whose opponents are career politicians and professional talkers. It is a foregone conclusion that they will beat him in a debate, but does this say anything about their ability to achieve real change or create jobs?

Trump: "I am not politically correct"

Trump is also on record as having made some very offensive comments about women. During a Republican primary debate in 2015 the moderator – Megan Kelly – draws his attention to these comments:

> Mr. Trump, one of the things people love about you is you speak your mind and you don't use a politician's filter. However, that is not without its downsides, in particular, when it comes to women. You've called women you don't like fat pigs, dogs, slobs, and disgusting animals. [...] Your Twitter account has several disparaging comments about women's looks. [...] Does that sound to you like the temperament of a man we should elect as president?

This is obviously an awkward question for Trump. A "yes" is, of course, no option, a "no" is also a very tricky answer – at least, from Trump's perspective. This is how Trump responds:

> I think the big problem
> this country has
> is being politically correct.
> I've been challenged by so many people,
> and I don't frankly have time for total political correctness.

> And to be honest with you,
> this country doesn't have time either.⁶

Trump does not enter into the frame by commenting on his disparaging statements. He responds with a meta-frame and says something about Kelly's question – the question sprouts from political correctness. Trump is not politically correct like other politicians and that his statements are simply a byproduct of his straight-talking nature. According to Trump, the issue is not whether he is a misogynist but that he has the courage to not be politically correct – and others do not have that courage.

Climate science deniers: "I am not a scientist"

Science and politics are often at odds, for example, when scientists release findings that undermine certain political positions. Politicians often resort to meta-framing in those types of situations. In the field of climate science, for example, there is almost unanimous consensus regarding the man-made causes of global warming. However, politicians who reject this view often say things like:

> I'm not a scientist.
> I am interested in protecting Kentucky's economy.
> I'm interested in having low cost electricity.⁷

or:

> Listen,
> I'm not qualified to debate the science over climate change.
> But I am astute enough to understand
> that every proposal that has come out of this administration
> to deal with climate change
> involves hurting our economy and killing American jobs.
> That can't be the prescription
> for dealing with changes in our climate.⁸

Scientists overwhelmingly agree that climate change is a man-made phenomenon, so politicians who reject this view often resort to meta-framing. "We are not scientists," they say, "so we cannot be expected to debate this issue with scientists." Instead, they look at the practical implications of measures designed to reduce global warming. If those measures have a negative impact on the economy, they argue that the measures themselves are defective.

A similar meta-frame exaggerates the level of disagreement within the scientific community. Instead of focusing on all the scientific evidence for global warming, this meta-frame says something general about the evidence itself. Because some scientists disagree with mainstream opinion, it argues, there is clearly no consensus on the question whether humans are responsible for global warming. Many economists will have a similar experience. When they, for example, criticize governments for their austerity policy, the simple but powerful reaction might be that economists disagree about the need for austerity policies. If scientists disagree, there clearly is no one right scientific answer to the question whether austerity works. And if the economic science does not have an answer, so why should we listen to an economist?

How to reframe?

When faced with a meta-frame, reframing is not that complicated. Simply stick to your original message – and say that your opponent is looking the other way. Frame a meta-frame as avoiding the real issue. John King could have asked again whether Gingrich proposed an open marriage or not. Tony Abbott could have said that Gillard's lecture about what he said in the past, is simply a strategy to avoid the real issue: a speaker using sexist language should go.

Again, there is the question of whether framing is merely a rhetorical trick, or whether it can contribute to the quality of political debates. The same conclusion as in the earlier chapters can be drawn here: meta-framing can indeed be nothing but a rhetorical trick, but it can also enrich the debate. The meta-frames of Gingrich and Gillard are smart rhetorical tricks, but they also add something to the debate that matters. They present, as is always the case with framing, a new perspective on the issues at stake. Whether people perceive this as a trick or an enrichment of the debate will in most cases depend on their political stances.

8. Emotion and monopolies on emotion

George Bush, Bill Clinton, Hillary Clinton and Angela Merkel, faced with emotions

This chapter examines three cases in which a politician comes face-to-face with a member of the public. In each example, the politician is presented with a deeply personal or emotionally charged question. Once I have presented all three cases, I will analyze the politicians' responses to these frames.

In the first, iconic example, George H. W. Bush and Bill Clinton are participating in a town-hall debate during the 1988 US presidential election. During the debate, a member of the audience – Marisa Hall Summers – asks them a question about the impact of the national debt on ordinary Americans.

> How has the national debt personally affected each of your lives?
> And if it hasn't,
> how can you honestly find a cure for the economic problems
> of the common people
> if you have no experience in what's ailing them?

She makes things even harder for the two candidates by suggesting that politicians who cannot identify with her situation will be incapable of adopting the right policies:

> I know people
> who cannot afford to pay the mortgage on their homes,
> their car payment.
> I have personal problems with the national debt.
> But how has it affected you
> and if you have no experience in it, how can you help us,
> if you don't know what we're feeling?[1]

In my second example, German chancellor Angela Merkel is participating in a televised debate with a group of young people. Reem Sahwil, a young girl from Lebanon who has been living in Germany for several years, asks Merkel whether she and her family will be allowed to stay there:

> I also have goals, just like other people. [...]
> I want to go to university.
> That is my wish, something I'd really like to achieve.
> It's really hard to watch other people enjoy life
> when you are unable to enjoy it with them.[2]

Reem puts a human face on Merkel's immigration policy. In Germany, as elsewhere, immigrants need to satisfy certain criteria and go through various procedures in order to be granted permanent residence. Reem, who speaks fluent German, has still not completed these procedures.

The third example is about Hillary Clinton. Clinton is competing in the Democratic primaries in 2015. At a town-hall meeting, a ten-year-old girl – Hannah Tandy – asks her the following question:

> What are you going to do
> about bullying?[3]

The lifeworld versus the system world and the monopoly on emotion

In the three examples, Bush, Merkel and the Clintons are each presented with an emotionally charged question that puts them in an awkward position. How do they respond to being placed in such an emotional frame?

First up is George Bush, who has a problem understanding the question. Asked how the national debt has affected him personally, he starts taking about interest rates and economic policy measures. He briefly addresses the question's personal dimension but then quickly resumes his overwhelmingly technocratic message:

> But I think in terms of the recession,
> of course you feel it when you're president of the United States.
> And that's why I'm trying to do something about it
> by stimulating the export, investing more, better education systems.

What is happening here? Bush, like the Clintons and Merkel, comes face-to-face with the collision of two very different worlds: the world of policy vs. the world of reality; the world of rules and procedures vs. the world of real people living real lives; or – as Habermas would put it – the world of systems vs. the lifeworld.[4]

When frames from these two worlds collide, the frame from the lifeworld is almost always stronger. Why is this? The lifeworld is always more tangible and accessible that the abstract ideas from systems world. More important, frames from the lifeworld are almost always grounded in emotion, which makes them warmer than frames from the world of systems. You empathize with Reem, who dreams about her future, and you share the concerns of Marisa Hall Summers, who cannot make ends meet. In contrast, the cold world of policy, procedures, abstract concepts, and systems hardly ever evokes an emotional response. Frames from the lifeworld therefore have a monopoly on emotion. This is what makes the position of Merkel, Bush, and the Clintons so difficult. They are obliged to defend the world of systems against questions from the lifeworld, which holds all the emotional cards.

Bush faces a question from the lifeworld but responds with an answer from the world of systems in which he talks about interest rates, exports, and investment. It is a very ineffective and weak response. His answer confirms that there is a deep gulf between the lifeworld and the world of systems – between the day-to-day life of the woman asking the question and the world of policy in Washington.

How to reframe?

If your opponent uses a frame from the lifeworld – thereby acquiring a monopoly on emotion – how do you reframe the debate? How do you establish a meaningful connection between the world of systems and the lifeworld? Finally, how do you seize the initiative from your opponent and shatter his or her monopoly?

The answer to these questions is that this can all be achieved in three steps:
1. Connect
2. Empathize
3. Highlight your values

Figure 15. Emotion and reframing

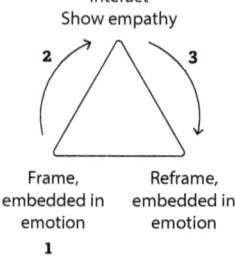

Connect

How does Hillary Clinton respond to Hannah's question about bullying? It is "Can you tell me a little bit more about why that's on your mind?" And how does Bill Clinton respond to Marisa Hall Summers's question about the impact of the national debt? It is "Tell me how it's affected you again. You know people who've lost their jobs and lost their homes?"

What is happening here? Instead of simply answering the question, Hillary and Bill both ask a personal question in return. By doing so, they establish an emotional connection with a person from the lifeworld. This connection transforms their status, they are no longer representatives of merely the world of systems.

Empathize

The discussion continues. Hannah responds to Hillary's question as follows: "I have asthma and occasionally I hear people talking behind my back." Hillary responds by saying:

> People can say something about somebody
> without having to look them in the eye
> or see them walk by,
> and so I think we all need to be aware
> of the pain and the real anguish that bullying can cause.

In the other debate, Bill now responds to the original question as follows:

> I'll tell you how it's affected me. [...]
> I have seen what's happened in [these] last four years.
> In my state, when people lose their jobs,
> there's a good chance I'll know them by their names.
> When a factory closes,
> I know the people who ran it.
> When the businesses go bankrupt,
> I know them.
> And I've been out here for thirteen months
> in meetings just like this,
> ever since October,
> with people like you all over America,
> people that have lost their jobs,
> lost their livelihood,
> lost their health insurance.

The main ingredient of both responses is a big dose of empathy. Hillary and Bill both show that they understand and identify with the situation of the questioner – that they share the same feelings and concerns.

Highlight your values

After making a connection and showing empathy, the third step in reframing the debate is to highlight the values that drive and inspire you – and the emotions inherent to these values. Let's see what the Clintons do next.

Hillary says,

> I really do think we need more love and kindness in our country.
> I think we are not treating each other
> with the respect and the care that we should show toward each other.
> And that's why it's important
> to stand up to bullies wherever we are,
> and why we shouldn't let anybody bully
> his way into the presidency,
> because that is not who we are as Americans.

And Bill says,

> What I want you to understand
> is the national debt is not the only cause of that.
> It is because America has not invested in its people. [...]
> Most people are working harder for less money
> than they were making ten years ago.
> It is because we are in the grip of a failed economic theory. [...]
> I think [what] we have to do is invest in American jobs,
> American education, control American health-care costs,
> and bring the American people together again.

Hillary wants a kinder and more respectful country that stands up to bullies. Bill wants to invest in the American people and bring them together again, not abandon them to a failed economic theory. It's clear that they are not just talking about policies but also – primarily – about the values underlying those policies, such as the importance of empowering people. Moreover, as discussed in Chapter 3, values are always linked to emotions. Anyone who is receptive to the Clintons' message about values will also experience a warm glow of emotion on hearing this message.

The right order

Connect, be empathetic, show the values that drive and inspire you. The Clintons both manage to reframe the debate when confronted with an emotionally charged frame. Angela Merkel faces a much tougher challenge in this regard. Her government is directly responsible for the policy that has resulted in Reem's long and agonizing wait to find out whether she and her family will be granted asylum. She, also, asks questions when Reem tells her about her dreams (Step 1: Connect) and then she responds as follows:

> Seeing you here before me,
> I can tell that you're a very likeable person.
> But you know that there are thousands and thousands of people
> in Palestinian refugee camps in Lebanon.
> If we were to tell them and everyone in Africa
> and everywhere else
> that they can all come to Germany
> we wouldn't be able to cope. This is our dilemma.
> And the only logical response
> is to say that we cannot take forever to make a decision.
> But some people will have to go back to where they came from.

Reem listens to the chancellor but suddenly bursts out crying. The situation has clearly become too upsetting for her. Merkel walks over to comfort Reem and says, "Ah, come on now. You did such a good job." She puts her hand on Reem's shoulder and continues, "because we don't want to put you in this kind of situation, and because you're having a tough time, and because you made it very clear to many, many others what kind of situation people can end up in."

What goes wrong here? Merkel asks questions (connect), but then she talks about her policy, followed by a more empathetic response. First of all, she could have changed the order of her response, by showing empathy (Step 2) after having connected by asking questions (Step 1).

Second, instead of a policy response, she could have answered by referring to her values. If she had managed to do so, she might have said something along the following lines, following Step 2 (showing empathy) and Step 3 (highlighting values):

> Seeing you here before me,
> I can tell that you're a very likeable and courageous person.
> And I understand everyone understands how difficult this is for you.
> How terrible it is that somebody your age is so worried about her future.
> Nobody begrudges you or any other child a carefree and happy life here in Germany.

Next, she could have highlighted her values:

> At the same time,
> everyone understands that we cannot accept
> an unlimited number of immigrants.
> Everyone knows we need to set limits.
> This means we will have to disappoint certain people.
> I want this to be a country where there are jobs for everyone.
> A country where people feel at home and live together in harmony.
> A country that is hospitable for people that have to fear for their lives.

However, if we want to be hospitable in the future, we need to set certain limits today.

What do we learn from this? As representatives of the world of systems, politicians should be able to speak from the heart and show emotion. That is why they should follow the three steps, when faced with emotional frames: connect, show empathy, show your own vales and emotions. This will, of course, not ensure that they win every debate – there are obviously too many factors at play to guarantee such an outcome – but it does prevent the other party from having a monopoly on emotion. When both parties share their values and emotions, the debate takes place on a level playing field. And don't forget: the order – interact, show empathy, emphasize your values – matters.

Populism and emotional frames

Many populist parties are very good in creating a monopoly on emotion. Here is Geert Wilders again, leader of the Dutch anti-immigration Freedom Party, talking about Islam: "Islam is a totalitarian ideology and the single greatest threat to our society."[5]

According to Wilders, the Netherlands's worst problems – and the solutions to those problems – are as follows:

Problem: Moroccan youths are throwing stones at the police. Solution: Arrest, prosecute, and deport them! Problem: The economy is shrinking even faster than the poll numbers of the Dutch Conservative Party. Solution: Curtail liberal pursuits like foreign aid, subsidies for disadvantaged neighborhoods, and public broadcasting, and give ordinary people their money back. Problem: The government is permitting record levels of immigration. Solution: Don't allow in any more Eastern Europeans and close the border to immigrants from Muslim countries. [...] Repatriation, repatriation, repatriation! What goes in, must come out![6]

How do mainstream politicians typically respond to such radical suggestions? They say things like:

> These solutions aren't feasible.
> You cannot deport young people just because they have a criminal record.
> We need Eastern European immigrants because there are no candidates for certain jobs.
> You cannot keep lowering taxes indefinitely.
> These solutions tar all Muslims with the same brush.
> A majority of Muslims are hard-working, upstanding citizens.

These responses are not always effective, because Wilders's suggestions are less about finding practical solutions and more about indirectly expressing underlying emotions – in this case anger regarding the delinquent behavior of young immigrants or the loss of jobs due to immigration. The rational responses listed above fail to acknowledge this anger and thus grant Wilders a monopoly on emotion. It is much more effective for his opponents to start with a show of empathy: "I am angry about the behavior of these young people." This message instantly challenges Wilders's emotional monopoly. The next step is to highlight the values that drive [and inspire] you, such as the belief that people should feel safe in their own neighborhoods. People who are scared cannot live normal lives, which is why – unlike Wilders – you intend to take measures that will be effective. Showing your values is showing emotions – which will at least result in a level playing field: neither Wilders nor his opponents have a monopoly on emotion.

In previous chapters, we have seen that reframing often improves the quality of political debate. The same applies here. When one party has a monopoly on emotion, it has a clear advantage in the arena of public opinion. This is because the lifeworld usually trumps the world of systems in such situations. However, if you reframe the debate by connecting, empathizing, and highlighting your values, you can level the playing field. This doesn't necessarily mean that you will win the debate, but it does mean that if you lose, it will not be solely down to the fact that your opponent had a monopoly on emotion.

Part Three

Reflection

9. How should we value the game of framing and reframing?

In this book, I hope to have shed some light on how the framing and reframing game is played. Unraveling the workings of this game enables us to better understand or better conduct debates, in the event that we ourselves must take the floor in a particular discussion.

An important question that remains is what value we should attach to the framing/reframing game? Certainly, many feel that framing is morally wrong – a trick that leads people astray from the reality.

Is framing morally wrong?

There are several answers to this question. I will leave it to you to decide which answers are right or wrong.

Answer 1: Framing is deceitful – and therefore morally repugnant.

Frames obscure the truth and lead to "fact-free politics" – a term coined by Bill Clinton. When politicians use frames, perception becomes more important than reality. Consider the debate on global warming. In scientific circles, there is almost unanimous agreement that climate change is a man-made phenomenon. Opponents of this view have nevertheless managed to activate a controversy frame by claiming that scientists fundamentally disagree on this issue. This is factually incorrect. There is actually widespread consensus on the man-made nature of global warming. As the American journalist H. L. Mencken once said: "For every complex problem there is an answer that is clear, simple, and wrong." A similar sentiment applies here – for every complex issue, there is a frame that is clear, simple and wrong.

Answer 2: Framing might be deceitful – but we have to frame.

Politics is a battle of ideas in which frames are used to win support for different views. If your opponents use frames, you cannot avoid doing so yourself. If you don't, you are no longer operating on a level playing field. As described above, opponents of man-made global warming have successfully used a controversy frame to undermine the scientific consensus on this issue. Conservative voters might be susceptible for this frame, since they stand for business values and more climate change policies might result in more regulation for businesses. Anyone seeking support for policies addressing climate change therefore also needs to activate powerful frames, for example, by claiming that action against climate change is a path to economic development and growth and will create new business opportunities. Framing may be morally wrong, but in some situations you cannot get away from it, especially if you are fighting for what you believe to be a good cause.

Answer 3: Framing versus reality? There is no distinction between reality and framing.

In politics, almost every issue is open to multiple interpretations: there is no objective reality. As a result, there is no single way to discuss an issue. For instance, is a person who lives and works in a foreign country without proper papers an "illegal immigrant" or an "undocumented worker"? The answer to this question generally depends on your political affiliation. If you are conservative, you are likely to describe this person as an illegal immigrant and condemn the other term as a frame that is designed to obscure the reality of the situation. If you are more liberal, you are liable to take the opposite approach. It is not framing versus reality, a frame is merely a perspective on the reality – and a reframe is another perspective on the same reality.

Answer 4: Framing is a moral obligation.

As noted above, supporters of action on global warming rely may have to develop frames to cope with their opponents' framing – making framing a kind of necessary evil. However, when there is no distinction between a frame and reality, framing stops being a necessary evil and becomes a moral obligation. If you believe that the world is in grave danger from global warming – and that humanity has a moral responsibility to do something about it – but then ignore the need to use effective frames to achieve your goals, you are not living up to your moral obligations.

Answer 5: Framing is a democratic duty.

This answer is closely related to answer 4. In a democracy, legitimacy is a key value and public support is therefore crucial in the process of policy making. However, because social problems are often very complicated, policy is often very complex, too. Politicians therefore have a duty to explain their policies in a clear manner and reduce complex issues to their essence – and that is what a frame does. Consider the conservative frame regarding development aid – "Don't give poor people fish: teach them how to fish." You could write this off as a shallow slogan or a mean-spirited frame, but a conservative politician could argue just as easily that this is the true essence of his policy: it is much better to empower people than to make them dependent on government handouts. If you disagree with it, you should seek to articulate the essence of your own position on development aid instead of complaining that your opponent is using frames. The public will then have a choice between two viewpoints that have been reduced to their essence.

Answer 6: Framing acts as a heuristic for good policy.

Since framing is partly about reducing political ideas to their essence, it can also play a key role in the policy-making process. When a politician is unable to find a good frame to communicate a policy, it raises the question whether the policy itself is any good. Policies are often the result of multiparty negotiations in which the search for consensus ends up taking precedence over quality. In such situations, it is often useful to adopt a framing-based perspective. Is it possible to explain the resulting policy in clear and concise terms? If you are unable to find a good frame to communicate your policy, the policy itself may be at fault.

Answer 7: Framing contributes to the quality of the political debate.

If a frame and a reframe are merely different perspectives of the same reality, then the game of framing and reframing can effectively contribute to the quality of the political debate. In politics, we deal with wicked problems, for which there is no single solution. Therefore, it is beneficial to the quality of the decision-making process that a variety of perspectives are introduced. The lesson from Chapter 3-8 was that through the game of framing and reframing, more perspectives are brought to light to the political debate.

So, is framing morally wrong? As noted above, it is up to you to decide which answer you agree with most. This will most likely depend on the issue in question. In some cases framing may seem deceitful, while in others it may feel like a moral obligation or contribute to the quality of political decision-making. The answer to the morality question often also depends on your political beliefs and affiliations: one person's immoral frame is another person's honest opinion.

A simple frame versus a complex reality

Finally, one question remains. I have often noticed a tension between the simple frame and the complex reality. How should we value this tension?

To make this clear, I would like to refer back to an example from Chapter 4 – on the victim-villain-hero frame. In Chapter 4, I gave the example of the daddy tax. There are young fathers who pay no attention to the children they fathered. The entire burden of childrearing falls upon the young mothers. The fathers receive an unemployment benefit, and our daddy tax politician wants to levy a 100 percent tax on this benefit and pay this money to the mothers. This creates a villain (the fathers), a victim (the mothers) and a hero (the daddy tax politician).

One the one hand, the daddy tax is a powerful frame, because of the underlying division of roles and the emotions the issue evokes. On the other hand, in practice it is completely ineffective: it cannot be legally enforced, and the fathers can simply deny paternity. So there is a tension between the simple frame and the complex reality. How should we value this tension?

Two mindsets

The reality can sometimes be hugely complex – a problem has many causes, several solutions are available, all these solutions have side effects, some of which are undesirable. Our societies are also very dynamic, which means that the problems and solutions of today may be obsolete tomorrow – which makes problem solving an even more complex endeavor.

Politicians are faced with at least two mindsets:
- The *analytical mindset*: The analysis of a problem and the design of a solution, which demands a high tolerance for complexity
- The *communicative mindset*: Explaining the essence of problems and solutions to the wider public, which requires the competency to provide sense and simplicity

A thought experiment. Suppose you have a neighborhood with a high crime rate. A politician explains that this is a complex issue. There happens to be a lot of poverty in the neighborhood, and many of the young people are educationally disadvantaged. Even supposing that that is all true – the question still arises: What do we hear when a politician pronounces that a problem is complex? What feelings does that evoke? Politicians who constantly address a problem in terms of its complexity, give the impression that they are not in control, are not able to solve the problem – or maybe they are not even willing to solve the problem. It is not what you say (the problem is complex), it is what people hear (they cannot and will not solve the problem).

So there is a need to reduce complexity to a concise message or, put differently, a frame that inspires or convinces the audience – and this reduction is by definition debatable. Frames are necessary, but inherently simple or, depending on your political stance, too simple. There is even a paradox here. The more complex and dynamic the reality, the higher the tolerance of complexity politicians need – but at the same time: the higher the need for a concise message that provides us with sense and simplicity. Put differently, the more complex problems are, the more simplicity we need – and the more we need powerful frames. Politicians with good frames will more easily get a license to act from us, a license to develop policies – maybe even other policies than they originally proposed.

Notes

1. **Language matters**
   1. *The West Wing*, season 5, episode 92.
   2. Thibodeau and Boroditsky (2011).
   3. Greenberg (1996). See also Greenberg (2008).
   4. De Bruijn (2011).
   5. Parker-Pope (2013); Esserman, Thompson and Reid (2013).
   6. Bowman (2014).
   7. Carter (1996).
   8. Boehner (2010).
   9. White House (2015).
   10. Smit (2010).
   11. Kuypers (2009), Van Gorp (2006), Lakoff (2004), Lakoff (2008).
   12. Chong and Druckman (2007) define "filter" and "message" as "internal" and "external" frame, respectively.
   13. See, for example, Entman's (1993) definition of framing: "to select some aspects of a perceived reality and make them more salient in a communicating text, in such a way as to promote a particular problem definition, causal interpretation, moral evaluation, and/or treatment recommendation."
   14. Scheufele and Iyengar (2012).
   15. Schön and Rein (1994), p. 32. The term "frame" is used in a variety of disciplines, often with slightly different meaning in each one. For an overview of definitions, see Van Gorp (2006).

2. **What is framing and how does it work?**
   1. Accessible publications on framing include: Lakoff (2004), Fairhurst (2011), Jones (2010). More indirect about framing, but interesting, is Denning (2007).
   2. Van Lieshout, Went and Kremer (2010), p. 108.
   3. Gladwell (2002), pp. 89-132.
   4. Mankiw (2015).
   5. Price, Tewksbury and Powers (1997).
   6. Truijens (2016).
   7. De Bruijn (2011).
   8. *Der Spiegel* (2010).

9. Sander Dekker, the Dutch education minister, speaking on 17 March 2013 on *Buitenhof*, a Sunday morning political interview television program.
10. Lakoff (2004), pp. 3-4.
11. Ibid., p. 3.
12. Siegel (2010).
13. Torry (2014).
14. Makarechi (2016).
15. Rosenberg and Schmitt (2017).
16. Ibid.
17. Baker and Davis (as 2017).
18. This debate took place on 23 May 2010.
19. Lakoff (2004).
20. Scheuer (1999).
21. Arthur C. Brooks in his review of Mankiw (2015).

3. The 3P model
1. Collins (2010).
2. Mankiw (2015).
3. Ibid.
4. Clinton (1996), pp. 1829-1834.
5. Republican National Committee (2013), p. 7.
6. Ibid.
7. Frank (2004).
8. Hochschild (2018).
9. Quoted in *New York Times* (1992).2
10. There is, of course, a strong similarity here to Aristotle's logos, pathos, and ethos.
11. Quoted in Spilakos (2014).
12. Lewis (1987).
13. Quoted in Westen (2007).
14. See the analysis of this exchange in Westen (2007).
15. Transcript of the Republican presidential debate in Houston (2016).
16. Dathan (2015).
17. Egan (2010).

4. **Victims, villains, and heroes**
1. Effting and Meerhof (2005).
2. This model is discussed in many publications about framing: Van Gorp (2006), Czarniawska (1997), Van Eeten (1999), Jones (2010), Lakoff (2008).
3. Sloterdijk (2010).
4. Scruton (2010).
5. Moïsi (2009).
6. Wilders (2009).
7. Australian health Minister Peter Dutton, quoted in Maiden (2013).
8. Luntz (2007).
9. Jenninger (1988).
10. *Der Spiegel* (1988).
11. Gentilviso (2010). See also Baker (2010b).
12. Rudd (2013).
13. Jeroen Dijsselbloem, quoted in several media, 2013.

5. **Playing with your opponent's values**
1. Quoted in UK Parliament (1990).
2. Ibid.
3. Rubio (2013).
4. Wikipedia (2018).

6. **Playing with opposite perspectives**
1. Walker (2017).
2. De Bruijn (2012).
3. Baker (2010a).
4. Elbaradei (2013).
5. Clinton (2012).
6. Cameron (2010).

7. **Meta-framing**
1. Spillius (2012).
2. Gillard (2012).
3. Presidential Campaign Debate of September 23, 1976, p. 2296.
4. Bush (1988).
5. *ABC News* (2015).
6. Ross (2015).
7. Cama (2014).
8. McCarthy (2014).

8. **Emotion and monopolies on emotion**
1. Swaine (2012).
2. Noack (2015).
3. Leys (2015).
4. Habermas (1984).
5. De Bruijn (2011).
6. Proceedings of the Dutch House of Representatives, Continuation of the debate on the 2008 Annual Reports and the Reports of the Netherlands Court of Audit (31924) and the Government's Progress Report on its 2008 Policy Program (31951), May 28, 2009 (in Dutch).

References

ABC News (2015) Donald Trump: "I'm not a debater." [Video clip], 8 February. http://abcnews.go.com/ThisWeek/video/donald-trump-im-debater-32836860.

Baker, Peter (2010a) Education of a president. *New York Times*, 12 October. https://www.nytimes.com/2010/10/17/magazine/17obama-t.html.

Baker, Peter (2010b) Elitism takes root as Republican mantra. *International Herald Tribune*, 1 November.

Baker, Peter, and Julie Hirschfeld Davis (2017) Trump defends sharing information on ISIS threat with Russia. *New York Times*, 16 May. https://www.nytimes.com/2017/05/16/us/politics/trump-intelligence-russia-classified.html.

Boehner, John (2010) Transcript of interview. *Politics Daily*, 13 December.

Bowman, Sam (2014) The Negative Income Tax and Basic Income are pretty much the same. *Adam Smith Institute blog*, 25 May. https://www.adamsmith.org/blog/welfare-pensions/the-negative-income-tax-and-basic-income-are-pretty-much-the-same-thing.

Bush, George H. W. (1988) Acceptance speech at the Republican National Convention, 18 August.

Cama, Timothy (2014) McConnell dodges on climate change. *The Hill*, 3 October. https://thehill.com/policy/energy-environment/219676-sen-mcconnell-on-climate-change-im-not-a-scientist.

Cameron, David (2010) Address at the Munich Security Conference, 5 February.

Carter, Jimmy (1996,) *Living Faith*. New York: Random House.

Chong, D., and J. N. Druckman (2007) Framing theory. *Annual Review of Political Science* 10, pp. 103-126.

Clinton, Bill (2012) Transcript of Bill Clinton's speech to the Democratic National Convention. *New York Times*, 5 September. https://www.nytimes.com/2012/09/05/us/politics/transcript-of-bill-clintons-speech-to-the-democratic-national-convention.html.

Clinton, William J. (1996) Remarks at the Kennedy-King Dinner in Alexandria, Virginia, October 21 1994. In *Public Papers of the Presidents of the United States: William J. Clinton, 1994: August 1 to December 31, 1994*. Washington, DC: Government Printing Office, pp. 1829-1832.

Collins, Gail (2010) A state of two minds. *New York Times*, 17 September. https://www.nytimes.com/2010/09/18/opinion/18collins.html.

Czarniawska, Barbara (1997) *Narrating the Organization. Dramas of Institutional Identity*. Chicago: University of Chicago Press.

Dathan, Matt (2015) David Cameron and Boris Johnson told they're elitist and out of touch because they went to Eton, *The Independent*, 5 May. https://www.independent.co.uk/news/uk/politics/generalelection/general-election-2015-watch-david-cameron-and-boris-johnson-being-told-theyre-elitist-and-out-of-10226546.html.

De Bruijn, Hans (2011) *Geert Wilders Speaks Out: The Rhetorical Frames of a European Populist*. The Hague: Eleven International.

De Bruijn, Hans (2012), Januskop van Rutte past ons allemaal. Trouw 6 July. https://www.trouw.nl/opinie/januskop-van-rutte-past-ons-allemaal~a7eae7ae/

Denning, Stephen (2007) *The Secret Language of Leadership*, San Francisco: Wiley.

Der Spiegel (1988) "Mit Knobelbechern durch die Geschichte." 14 November. http://www.spiegel.de/spiegel/print/d-13530781.html.

Der Spiegel (2010) Kandidat Gauck soll Wulff Stimmen abjagen. 4 June. http://www.spiegel.de/politik/deutschland/bundespraesidenten-duell-kandidat-gauck-soll-wulff-stimmen-abjagen-a-698737.html.

Effting, Maud, and Ron Meerhof (2005) Antillianen zijn dé prioriteit. *De Volkskrant*, 19 November. https://www.volkskrant.nl/nieuws-achtergrond/antillianen-zijn-de-prioriteit~b6cd8582/.

Egan, Timothy (2010) A big idea. *New York Times*, 6 December. https://opinionator.blogs.nytimes.com/2010/12/06/a-big-idea/.

Elbaradei, Mohamed (2013) You can't eat Sharia. *Foreign Policy*, 24 June.

Entman, R. M. (1993). Framing: Towards clarification of a fractured paradigm. In D. McQuail, ed., *McQuail's Reader in Mass Communication Theory*. Thousand Oaks: SAGE Publications, pp. 390-397.

Esserman, Laura J., Ian M. Thompson, and Brian Reid (2013) Overdiagnosis and overtreatment in cancer: An opportunity for improvement. *Journal of the American Medical Association* 310(8), pp. 797-798.

Fairhurst, Gail T. (2011) *The Power of Framing: Creating the Language of Leadership*. San Francisco: Wiley.

Frank, Thomas (2004) *What's the Matter with Kansas? How Conservatives Won the Heart of America*. New York: Holt.

Gentilviso, Chris (2010) U.S. President Barack Obama on the country's electorate. *Time*, 18 October.

Gillard, Julia (2012) Transcript of speech. *Sydney Morning Herald*, 10 October.

Gladwell, Malcolm (2002) *The Tipping Point: How Little Things Can Make a Big Difference*. Boston: Little Brown.

Greenberg, Stanley B. (1996) *Middle Class Dreams: Politics and Power of the New American Majority*. New York: Times Books.

Greenberg, Stanley B. (2008) Goodbye, Reagan Democrats. *New York Times*, 10 November. https://www.nytimes.com/2008/11/11/opinion/11greenberg.html.

Habermas, Jürgen (1984) *Theory of Communicative Action*. Boston: Beacon Press.

Hochschild, Arlie R. (2018) *Strangers in Their Own Land: Anger and Mourning on the American Right*. New York: The New Press.

Jenninger, Philipp (1988) Rede am 10. November 1988 im Deutschen Bundestag.

Jones, Michael D. (2010) *Heroes and Villains: Cultural Narratives, Mass Opinions and Climate Change*. PhD diss., University of Oklahoma.

Kuypers, Jim A. (2009) *Rhetorical Criticism: Perspectives in Action*. Idaho Falls: Lexington Books.

Lakoff, George (2004) *Don't Think of an Elephant: Know Your Values and Frame the Debate*. White River Junction: Chelsea Green Publishing.

Lakoff, George (2008) *The Political Mind*. New York: Viking.

Lewis, William F. (1987) Telling America's story: Narrative form and the Reagan presidency. *Quarterly Journal of Speech* 73(3), pp. 280-302.

Leys, Tony (2015) Did Trump impugn fifth-grader's question to Clinton? *Des Moines Register*, 24 December.

Luntz, Frank (2007) *Words That Work: It's Not What You Say, It's What People Hear*. New York: Hyperion.

Maiden, Samantha (2013) Job cuts loom for army of health bureaucrats, *Sunday Telegraph*, 22 September.

Makarechi, Kia (2016) Donald Trump admits he lost Iowa because he has no idea how to run a campaign. *Vanity Fair*, 3 February.

Mankiw, Gregory N. (2015) "The Conservative Heart," by Arthur C. Brooks. *New York Times*, 28 July. https://www.nytimes.com/2015/08/02/books/review/the-conservative-heart-by-arthur-c-brooks.html.

McCarthy, Tom (2014) Meet the Republicans in Congress who don't believe climate change is real. *The Guardian*, 17 November. https://www.theguardian.com/environment/2014/nov/17/climate-change-denial-scepticism-republicans-congress.

Moïsi, Dominique, (2009) *The Geopolitics of Emotion: How Cultures of Fear, Humiliation, and Hope Are Reshaping the World*. New York: Anchor Books.

New York Times (1992) The 1992 Campaign: Verbatim; Heckler stirs Clinton anger: Excerpts from the exchange. 28 March. https://www.nytimes.com/1992/03/28/us/1992-campaign-verbatim-heckler-stirs-clinton-anger-excerpts-exchange.html.

Noack, Rick (2015) Watch: Germany's Merkel makes a young refugee girl cry, then tries to comfort her. *The Washington Post*, 16 July.

Parker-Pope, Tara (2013) Scientists seek to rein in diagnoses of cancer. *New York Times*, 30 July. https://well.blogs.nytimes.com/2013/07/29/report-suggests-sweeping-changes-to-cancer-detection-and-treatment/.

Presidential Campaign Debate of September 23, 1976 (1979). In *Public Papers of the Presidents of the United States: Gerald R. Ford, 1976-1977,*. Washington, DC: Government Printing Office, pp. 2283-2312.

Price, Vincent, David Tewksbury and Elisabeth Powers (1997) Switching trains of thought: The impact of news frames on readers' cognitive responses. *Communication Research* 24(5), pp. 481-506.

Republican National Committee (2013) Growth & Opportunity Project. http://online.wsj.com/public/resources/documents/RNCreport03182013.pdf.

Rosenberg, Matthew, and Eric Schmitt (2017) Trump revealed highly classified intelligence to Russia, in break with ally, officials say. *New York Times*, 15 May. https://www.nytimes.com/2017/05/15/us/politics/trump-russia-classified-information-isis.html.

Ross, Janell (2015) So which women has Donald Trump called 'dogs' and 'fat pigs'? *The Washington Post*, 8 August.

Rubio, Marco (2013) Rubio addresses conservatives on immigration reform. *Marco Rubio: US Senator for Florida* website, 26 June. https://www.rubio.senate.gov/public/index.cfm/press-releases?ID=fa619075-cd59-4736-9234-a57165d6bod6.

Rudd, Kevin (2013) Transcript of broadcast on the Regional Resettlement Arrangement between Australia and PNG. *PM Transcripts: Transcripts from the Prime Ministers of Australia*, 19 July. http://pmtranscripts.pmc.gov.au/taxonomy/term/13?page=2.

Scheuer, Jeffrey (1999) *The Sound Bite Society: Television and the American Mind*. New York: Four Walls and Eight Windows.

Scheufele, D. A., and S. Iyengar (2012) *The State of Framing Research: A Call For New Directions*. New York: Oxford University Press.

Schön, Donald A., and Martin Rein (1994) *Frame Reflection: Toward the Resolution of Intractable Policy Controversies*. New York: Basic Books.

Scruton, Roger (2010) *The Uses of Pessimism: And the Danger of False Hope*. Oxford: Oxford University Press.

Siegel, Elyse (2010) Christine O'Donnell in new ad: "I'm not a witch." *Huffington Post*, 4 October. https://www.huffingtonpost.com/2010/10/04/christine-odonnell-witch-ad_n_750140.html.

Sloterdijk, Peter (2010) *Rage and Time: A Psychopolitical Investigation*. New York: Columbia University Press.

Smit, Jeroen (2010) *The Perfect Prey: The Fall of ABN Amro, or: What Went Wrong in the Banking Industry?* London: Quercus.

Spilakos, Peter (2014) We could use a Reagan, but which Reagan? *National Review*, 14 June. https://www.nationalreview.com/postmodern-conservative/we-could-use-reagan-which-reagan-peter-spiliakos//.

Spillius, Alex (2012) US election 2012: Newt Gingrich hits back at "open marriage" allegations. *The Telegraph*, 20 January. https://www.telegraph.co.uk/news/worldnews/us-election/9026858/US-election-2012-Newt-Gingrich-hits-back-at-open-marriage-allegations.html.

Swaine, John (2012) US Election: 1992 voter who stumped George HW Bush at debate criticises Mitt Romney. *The Telegraph*, 17 October.

Thibodeau, Paul H., and Lera Boroditsky (2011) Metaphors we think with: The role of metaphor in reasoning. *PLoS ONE* 6(2). https://doi.org/10.1371/journal.pone.0016782.

Torry, Harriet (2014) France "not sick child of Europe" PM Manuel Valls tells Germany. *Wall Street Journal*, 22 September.

Transcript of the Republican presidential debate in Houston (2016) *New York Times*, 26 February. https://www.nytimes.com/2016/02/26/us/politics/transcript-of-the-republican-presidential-debate-in-houston.html.

Truijens, Aleid (2016) Rijke ouders lappen misgelopen stufi toch wel. *De Volkskrant*, 23 April. https://www.volkskrant.nl/nieuws-achtergrond/rijke-ouders-lappen-misgelopen-stufi-toch-wel~b0848868/.

UK Parliament (1990) *House of Commons Debates*, 22 November. https://publications.parliament.uk/pa/cm199091/cmhansrd/1990-11-22/Debate-3.html.

Van Eeten, Michel (1999) *Dialogues of the Deaf: Defining New Agendas for Environmental Deadlocks*. Delft: Eburon.

Van Gorp, Baldwin (2006) *Framing Asiel. Indringers en slachtoffers*, Leuven: Acco.

Van Lieshout, Peter, Robert Went, Monique Kremer (2010) *Less Pretension, More Ambition: Development Policy in Times of Globalization*. Amsterdam: Amsterdam University Press.

Walker, Peter (2017) May defends decision to seek close ties with Donald Trump. *The Guardian*, 1 February. https://www.theguardian.com/politics/2017/feb/01/theresa-may-defends-decision-seek-close-ties-donald-trump-pmqs.

Westen, Drew (2007) *The Political Brain: The Role of Emotion in Deciding the Fate of the Nation*. New York: Public Affairs.

The West Wing. Season 5, episode 92.

White House (2015) Statement by the Press Secretary on the murder of Egyptian citizens, 15 February. https://obamawhitehouse.archives.gov/the-press-office/2015/02/15/statement-press-secretary-murder-egyptian-citizens.

Wilders, Geert (2009) Speech to CPAC Conference, 1 March, Omni Shoreham Hotel, Washington, DC.

Wikipedia (2018) Bear in the woods, 14 December. https://en.wikipedia.org/wiki/Bear_in_the_woods.

For Product Safety Concerns and Information please contact our EU representative GPSR@taylorandfrancis.com
Taylor & Francis Verlag GmbH, Kaufingerstraße 24, 80331 München, Germany

www.ingramcontent.com/pod-product-compliance
Lightning Source LLC
Chambersburg PA
CBHW070919180426
43192CB00038B/1964